The Supernatural: From ESP to UFOs

MELVIN BERGER

The John Day Company
New York

Copyright © 1977 by Melvin Berger
All rights reserved. Except for use in a review, the reproduction or utilization of this work in any form or by any electronic, mechanical, or other means, now known or hereafter invented, including xerography, photocopying, and recording, and in any information storage and retrieval system is forbidden without the written permission of the publisher. Published simultaneously in Canada by Fitzhenry & Whiteside Limited, Toronto.
Manufactured in the United States of America
Designed by Amy Hill

Library of Congress Cataloging in Publication Data
Berger, Melvin. The supernatural. Bibliography: p. Includes index. SUMMARY: Discusses ESP, parapsychology, astrology, psychokinesis, spiritualism, faith healing, witchcraft, and UFO's. 1. Psychical research—Juvenile literature. 2. Occult sciences—Juvenile literature. [1. Occult sciences. 2. Psychical research] I. Title. BF1031.B43 133 77-2829
ISBN 0-381-90054-1

10 9 8 7 6 5 4 3

THE SUPERNATURAL: FROM ESP TO UFOs

133
Ber

BOOKS BY MELVIN BERGER

Those Amazing Computers!
Uses of Modern Thinking Machines

The Supernatural: From ESP to UFOs

In the Scientists at Work *series*

South Pole Station
The National Weather Service
Animal Hospital
Oceanography Lab
Pollution Lab
Cancer Lab
Consumer Protection Labs
Police Lab
Medical Center Lab

053877

CONTENTS

1 A Personal Preface   1
2 ESP   4
3 Parapsychology   16
4 Astrology   30
5 Psychokinesis   47
6 Spiritualism   60
7 Faith Healing   75
8 Witchcraft   83
9 UFOs   99
  Some Books of Interest   108
  Some Addresses of Interest   112
  Index   115

THE SUPERNATURAL: FROM ESP TO UFOs

A PERSONAL PREFACE

One summer evening, many years ago, I visited an art gallery in Provincetown, Massachusetts, at the tip of Cape Cod. As I stood looking at one of the paintings, a gentleman approached me:

"That's my painting," he said. "Do you like it?"

"Yes," I said, wondering why he was looking at me in such a peculiar way.

"You grew up in Brooklyn, New York, didn't you?" he asked next.

"That's right," I answered, trying hard to remember him from my youth. "Did you?"

"No," he said, and then went on, "you lived in the neighborhood around 11th Street, didn't you?"

"Yes, but how did you know?" I answered, still struggling to recall him.

"And you attended Public School 225."

"Yes, I did," I stammered, amazed that he could know so much about me when I did not know him at all.

"Your birthday is in August," he continued. "August 23rd to be exact."

Now I was entirely confused. Only my closest friends and relations knew my birthday. I insisted that he tell me how he happened to have this information.

He explained that he has a special ability to receive mental messages from certain people. From the moment he entered the room, he claimed, he began to receive these messages from me.

He continued to give me more information. "Your father was an upholsterer. You own two cars; they are both black. One is an American car; the other is German—a Mercedes, I think."

I shook my head, in assent and in wonderment. It was hard to believe that he was receiving my mental messages. But it was even harder to find any other explanation.

That strange and disquieting experience set me on a quest to learn more about the supernatural and the occult. Over the years I spoke to many people involved with the supernatural, from astrologers to witches, including those who claim to read minds, to see into the future, and to communicate with the dead.

I read many reports on unexplained happenings from

3 A Personal Preface

all over the world. I met with scientists who do laboratory research on the occult. And I studied material on illusion and trickery written by professional magicians.

This book presents the results of my research. I found that a good number of so-called supernatural occurrences were really just examples of coincidence, human error, or poor reporting. An even greater number were out-and-out tricks or frauds.

But there were also a large number, including my own experience in the Provincetown art gallery, that could not be explained in any of these ways. Are these occurrences really natural events that are just beyond our present understanding? Or do they show the existence of supernatural forces and powers?

These are big and important questions. I hope that this book will help you to discover the answers for yourself.

ESP

ESP: *Extrasensory perception, or receiving information without the use of any of the five senses.*

King Croesus, who ruled some 2,500 years ago in ancient Lydia, in what is now Asia Minor, had a vision that his son would soon be murdered. The vision came true, but in a strange way. According to accounts, the King hired a guard to protect his son. The guard, though, turned out to be the murderer, and he killed the young Prince, fulfilling the tragic prophecy.

In 456 B.C., a seer forecast that the Greek poet Aeschylus would be killed by an object falling from above. For safety, Aeschylus went to live in an open field. On the day foretold for his death, an eagle flying overhead flung down a large turtle it had captured, attempting to break open its shell. The turtle landed hard on Aeschylus's head, and the poet was killed.

5 ESP

Giuseppe Garibaldi, the great nineteenth-century Italian patriot, formed a mental picture of his mother's death while out at sea one time. When he returned to land, he learned to his horror that his mother had indeed died in his absence.

The American humorist, Mark Twain, was working on a Mississippi steamboat in 1858 when he had a vision of his brother Henry laid out in a metal coffin. He was dressed in one of Twain's suits, and had a bouquet of flowers on his chest, with one red rose in the center. A few days later when Mark Twain docked in Memphis, he was told that Henry had been killed in an explosion. Twain went to see the body. Henry was in a metal coffin, and was dressed in one of the author's suits. But there were no flowers. Then, while Twain was grieving, a woman entered the room carrying a bouquet of flowers. She placed the bouquet, including a red rose, on Henry's chest.

Early in April 1865, Abraham Lincoln told his wife and some friends of a dream he had. In this dream, he awoke to the sound of sobbing people. Following the sounds of crying, he came to the East Room of the White House, where several soldiers were standing guard around an open coffin. Many people were openly crying. Lincoln asked the soldiers who had died. "The President," one soldier replied, "killed by an assassin." A little later that month, President Lincoln was actually cut down by an assassin's bullet.

6 ESP

Luther Burbank, the brilliant plant scientist, claimed that he received messages from his sister, who lived far away, and from his dead mother.

The author Upton Sinclair reported many successes in transmitting drawings and pictures by thought alone. He described the results of his experiments in his 1930 book *Mental Radio*. The book so impressed Albert Einstein, one of the greatest scientists of all time, that he translated it into German.

Sigmund Freud, who is famous for his discovery of the unconscious and the development of psychoanalysis, explained psychic visions as hallucinations that came from childhood sexual tensions. Near the end of his life, though, he wrote: "If I had my life to live over again, I should devote myself to psychical research, rather than psychoanalysis."

Perception: Sensory and Extrasensory

In these various accounts of well-known people, information is received in out-of-the-ordinary ways. Information is usually received through one or more of our five senses—sight, sound, touch, smell and taste. Receiving information through our five senses is called sensory perception. Information that is received through a so-called "sixth-sense" is referred to as extrasensory perception, or ESP for short. Many more accounts could be given of public figures, people of great intelligence and ac-

7 ESP

complishment, who came to believe that information can be received by ESP.

No doubt you can also think of times that you received a message through a sixth sense. You know who is calling on the telephone before you pick up the phone; you feel someone staring at your back, you turn around and, sure enough, someone is staring at you; you get a feeling that someone you know is sick, and later find out that the person fell ill at that time.

Types of ESP

People have been reporting ESP experiences from the very beginning of recorded history. Most of these experiences fall into three main types.

The first type is often called mind reading. A more accurate name is telepathy. It is defined as communication between one mind and another, without using any of the five senses. When you know what a person is thinking, even though the person says or does nothing to give you a clue—that is telepathy.

The second type of ESP is commonly called second sight. It is better known as clairvoyance. The word comes from the French, and means clear seeing. Clairvoyance is the ability to "see" things or events when there is no possible way to see them by sight alone. If someone describes what is on a particular page of a closed book—that is clairvoyance.

The ability to foretell or forecast the future is another type of ESP. It is called precognition. In one famous example of precognition, a woman saw in a dream the front page of a newspaper that did not appear in print until two weeks later.

Sometimes other abilities are included in ESP. Clairaudience is the ability to hear voices or sounds that cannot be heard by the human sense of hearing. Psychokinesis, or telekinesis, is the ability to move or change objects by thought and will power only. And retrocognition is knowing about events that occurred in the past, without receiving information about these events in a normal way.

In recent years there have been accounts of several people who have shown remarkable ESP abilities. Peter Hurkos (born 1911) has been called in on many cases, and time after time has been able to describe or locate the criminal by his psychic powers. He dates these powers from June 1943, when he fell off a thirty-foot ladder in his native Holland, landing on his head. When he regained consciousness in the hospital three days later, he had a vision that another patient was really an English spy, and would be shot by the Germans on leaving the hospital. No one listened to him, and the Englishman was killed on the following day.

Hurkos finds that working on criminal cases exhausts him, leaving him sick for days. He now only accepts assignments of tracking down missing persons. He also gives public demonstrations of his psychic powers for college students.

But perhaps the best-known possessor of ESP abilities was Edgar Cayce (1877–1945). This thin, stooped, mild-looking man discovered his ESP at the age of twenty-four. He found he was able to put himself into a sleep-like trance and diagnose the illnesses of unknown people who might be thousands of miles away. Cayce was also able to prescribe treatment to cure the diseases. Most of his treatments went beyond those of traditional medicine. They included herbs, tonics, massages, special diets, electrical currents, and even "bedbug juice" for a case of dropsy. Mostly, the reports show that Cayce was correct both in his diagnosis and his cure.

As time went on, Cayce turned his powers to other matters. In his trances he began speaking about Christ, the Bible, reincarnation, lost civilizations, and other subjects concerned with mankind and the universe. All of these talks, called "readings," were carefully copied down, and are now preserved at the Association for Research and Enlightenment (ARE) in Virginia Beach, Virginia. There are presently some thirteen thousand ARE members who study Edgar Cayce's readings in small groups all over the country.

Despite the many reports of ESP over the centuries, not everyone believes that ESP really exists. Some hold that many examples of ESP are just coincidences. Thoughts, visions, hunches, and dreams occur all the time, they say. Over a long enough period of time, some of them are bound to be realized. Further, the ones that come true are reported and remembered. Those that fail to come true are quickly forgotten.

Others claim that a number of ESP experiences stem from sensory cues. Sensory cues are sights, sounds, or smells in the environment that are picked up by your senses, signals sometimes so faint that you are not consciously aware of them.

A weak smell, a quick glimpse, a soft sound are sensory cues that bring you information that you may attribute to ESP. A whiff of burning, so faint that you are not aware that you smelled anything, may make you run into the kitchen and catch the food just before it burns. A glimpse out of the corner of your eye, so fleeting that you do not realize that you have seen anything, might give you the feeling that someone is behind you. The barely heard sound of a radio or phonograph may lead you and someone else nearby to start whistling the same song at the same time.

Still others claim that many reports of ESP experiences are simply honest mistakes. You have a vague hunch that you will have a bad day. Later, when you lose your wallet, you are convinced that you knew that you would lose some money that day. Or you dream about an event after it has taken place. In time, you begin to think that the dream came before the event.

Believers in ESP point to all the accounts of ESP through history and to their own experiences as proof that telepathy, clairvoyance, and precognition exist. They suggest that everyone has some ESP ability. But, they say, just as some people have good vision and others need glasses, so some people have stronger ESP than others. People with especially well-developed ESP are called psychics. According to the believers, only a few people are actually psychics.

11 ESP

Test Your ESP

There are some experiments that you can try with a friend to test each other's ESP or psychic ability.

Here is a way to find out how well you can receive telepathic messages. You will need two sheets of lined paper, and a deck of playing cards. Number both sheets of paper from 1 to 52. Give one to your friend and keep the other.

Place your friend at the opposite end of the room or behind a screen so that you cannot see the cards or what your friend is writing. Then he or she should look at the top card, write the color of that card—red or black—next to number 1, and try to send you the color by telepathy. As soon as the color comes to your mind, enter it on your paper. Go through the entire deck this way. Do not discuss your choices or compare any answers until you are finished.

Then, check to see how many of your guesses were right. By statistics, the average number of right guesses should be 26. If you score a few more or less than 26, that is not significant. But if you score very much higher (30 or more), this might be a sign of psychic ability.

Go through the deck the same way a few more times. Do you continue to score well above average? If you do, then write up a detailed report of the test, and send it to one of the parapsychology organizations listed at the end of the book. They are usually interested in reading of such experiments. One of them might want to test you further under laboratory conditions.

After testing your telepathy by guessing between

black and red cards, you might want to go on to a slightly more difficult test. This time, try to name the suit—heart, diamond, spade, or club—of each card. The statistical average for this test is 13 correct out of 52. You can make the test even more difficult by using only the numbered cards of the deck and guessing the number on each card, from 1 to 10. On the average, you should be right 4 times out of 40.

You and your friend should now reverse roles. Your friend should guess the cards, while you go through the deck and send the information by telepathy. Are there big differences between the scores? Is there any evidence that either of you has any special psychic ability?

There are other ways to test telepathic powers. Close your eyes as your friend draws a simple shape on a piece of paper. Then, on a separate paper, try to reproduce that drawing. Compare them. Did you draw the same or similar figure or shape? Reverse roles. How does your friend perform?

Do you score well on tests of clairvoyance? Give something of yours—a ring, pen, belt, or key—to a friend. Leave the room while your friend hides the object somewhere in the room. Return in a little while. Concentrate on the object. Do you receive a clairvoyant signal from the object that helps you see it, even though it is hidden?

To further test clairvoyance, you will need five cards—four black and one red. Ask your friend to place the cards face down on a table and mix them about. Concentrate on the red card. Turn over the card that you think is red. What color is it? Repeat this five times.

How many times do you succeed in turning over the red card? By pure chance you should be right once in every five tries.

You can test your ability in precognition on your own. On a memo pad keep a record of each thought, feeling, vision, or dream of a future event that you have over a period of a week. Jot down your prediction as soon as possible, and as clearly and exactly as you can. Later, review your predictions. If you find that you have some ability in precognition, you might want to get in touch with a premonition registry, which keeps official records of predictions or premonitions and sees whether or not they come true. (See end of book for addresses.)

Improve Your ESP Scores

Several ESP researchers from Duke University and the University of California at Los Angeles hold that it is impossible to improve your ESP ability. That may be so, but there are several ways you can improve your ESP test scores.

One way to raise your mental telepathy scores is to learn to use sensory cues. Ask a friend to choose an object while you are out of the room that you will try to locate when you return. When you come back, hold on to your friend's hand, with your fingers on his or her pulse, just above the wrist. Search for the object with your friend by your side. Ask your friend to concentrate on the location of the object, but to be sure not to push or pull you in any direction.

Try to receive any telepathic messages that lead you

toward the object. But also pay attention to any signs of tension in your friend's hand or changes in pulse rate. A slight tightening of muscles, a slight increase in pulse, may indicate that you are approaching the object. In this game it will help you to say aloud what you are thinking and doing. "I think the object is near this lamp. Could it be in the drawer of the table? Maybe it is behind the chair." This kind of commentary will bring forth stronger reactions from your guide. Does your telepathy score improve with sensory cues?

Of course, you can also improve your ESP success by deception as practiced by most professional magicians, who include ESP demonstrations in their acts. Even Kreskin, one of the most popular and successful mentalist magicians, as they are called, admits that 90 percent of his act is based on illusion and tricks and 10 percent on extrasensory perception.

There are over a hundred ways to create the illusion of ESP. Suppose, for example, you wish to identify an object that was selected, but that you did not see. You might prearrange a code of signals with a confederate who saw the object that was chosen. The confederate helps you name the object either by sending physical signals (touching parts of the body, moving the hands) or by sending verbal signals (using code words to transmit information). A confederate can also pass information gathered before the show. You can astound an audience by telling what this man has in his pocket, and what that woman is carrying in her purse.

Blindfolds are a popular device used by stage magicians. Most people do not realize how easy it is to see through a blindfold. You, too, can impress others by receiving a written message, even though you are blindfolded. Ask someone to blindfold you, and then to write a number or a color on a large piece of paper. You probably can see the message by sighting down along your nose. If not, try to move the blindfold by wrinkling your nose and blinking your eyes. If this does not work, you can adjust the blindfold by passing your hands over your eyes as you concentrate. If none of these tricks work, use a thinner material for the blindfold next time.

One amazing ESP trick to show clairvoyance involves only common sense. First, write the words "red, chair, rose, Washington, three" on a piece of paper. Fold it over twice, and place it under a book or dish. Then ask a friend to name a color, a piece of furniture, a flower, a capital city, and a number. Hand the folded piece of paper to your friend and compare your guesses to his or her choices. Probably you will find that you have three or four correct guesses because you chose the words that are usually the first to come into people's minds when asked those questions.

Whether you believe that ESP is a sixth sense, or whether you are convinced it is a fake and fraud, you must agree that it is a fascinating subject, worthy of much more study. And that is exactly what is happening in parapsychology laboratories across the country and around the world today.

PARAPSYCHOLOGY

PARAPSYCHOLOGY: *The scientific study of ESP under laboratory conditions.*

George Albert Smith and Douglas Blackburn were two young Englishmen who, around 1880, often demonstrated their ability to send thoughts from one to the other. Frequently these demonstrations of telepathy were held in public before people prominent in science and other fields.

In a typical situation, Smith sat in a chair, heavily blindfolded. Blackburn, at the opposite end of the room, silently read and memorized a sentence handed to him by an onlooker. Then Blackburn approached Smith, and holding on to both his hands, concentrated on transferring the memorized sentence to Smith. After a few minutes he released Smith's hands, and stepped behind the other man's chair.

Softly and hesitatingly, but with perfect accuracy, Smith recited aloud the sentence that he had received from Blackburn. The scientists and the skeptics watched carefully for any sign that Blackburn was telling Smith the sentence. They saw none. They were convinced that this was indeed a demonstration of telepathy.

Early Investigations

The demonstrations by Smith and Blackburn and others led to a growing interest in ESP, telepathy, and other similar psychic phenomena. In July 1882, a group of scientists and professors from Cambridge University in England organized the Society for Psychical Research (SPR) to study these and other unexplained happenings.

One of their first subjects of study was the telepathic communication between Blackburn and Smith. The two men were invited to London to demonstrate their abilities before a committee of the SPR. Smith's eyes were covered with pads of wool and a heavy, dark blindfold; his ears were stuffed with cotton and plugs of putty; and, in addition, he was covered from head to toe by two heavy blankets.

Frederic Myers, a school inspector and leader of the SPR, handed Blackburn a scribbled drawing of many criss-crossed lines. Blackburn studied the drawing to impress it on his mind. He also made several pencil copies of the drawing to help in the telepathy. Members of the SPR committee watched both men carefully to be sure there was no contact between them. They did not hear or see them exchange any signals or signs.

Ten minutes after Blackburn began studying the drawing, Smith stretched out a hand from under the blanket, and reached for a pencil on the table. Five minutes later, he threw off the blankets, raised the blindfold, and showed Myers and the others an almost identical copy of the original drawing.

The SPR issued a statement attesting to the fact that this was indeed a display of mental telepathy.

Over the following years, the investigators of psychic phenomena attempted to use more scientific experimental methods in their studies of telepathy. In one famous 1919–20 study at the University of Groningen in Holland, Professor H. J. W. F. Brugmans and two other members of the psychology department set up a tightly controlled experiment to test the telepathic ability of a student, A. Van Damm.

In one room, Van Damm was blindfolded and seated before a checkerboard with 48 squares. Each square was marked with a number and a letter.

In the room directly above Van Damm's, the professors had an identical checkerboard. They selected various squares by drawing pieces of paper with letters and numbers from a basket. After each selection, they willed Van Damm, by telepathy, to choose the square that they had chosen. The scientists were able to observe Van Damm's moves through two panes of glass set in the floor of their room and in the ceiling of his room.

Since there were 48 squares on the board, Van Damm had 1 chance in 48 of picking the same square as the scientists by pure chance. In his first run of 80 separate trials (each guess is a trial), Van Damm should have picked the same square about 2 times.

Out of the first 80 trials, though, Van Damm chose

the right box not 2 times, but 32 times! He was far above the expected number of correct guesses, or hits.

Further runs were tried. In one run of 187 trials, Van Damm scored 60 hits. By chance alone he should have had only about 4 hits.

The Van Damm experiments were acclaimed as the first striking demonstration of telepathy under controlled laboratory conditions. They seemed to provide proof of the existence of telepathy. They also pointed the way for the study of psychic phenomena under scientific conditions.

The Work of Dr. Rhine

Joseph Banks Rhine (born 1895) first became interested in ESP and spiritualism through a series of talks given by Sir Arthur Conan Doyle, the author of the Sherlock Holmes books. Later, as a biology teacher at Harvard University in 1926, he met William McDougall, a professor of psychology and past president of the American Society for Psychical Research.

One year later, when McDougall accepted a position at Duke University, at Durham, North Carolina, in order to do research in psychical matters, both Dr. Rhine and his wife Louisa, also a biologist, joined him at Duke to do similar work. Together they set up the Parapsychology Laboratory to conduct experiments in ESP and other phenomena under carefully controlled conditions. They coined the word "psi" to refer to all the psychic occurrences they would be studying.

In the early years, the Rhines worked out various tests

and experiments to measure psi abilities. They based their work on statistics. The average number of hits that they should expect in each experiment by pure chance was computed. This number was then compared to the number of hits obtained by the subjects. Subjects who scored much higher were assumed to have some sort of psi power.

The main tool used by the Rhines to test psi abilities was a set of Zener cards, or ESP cards, developed by Dr. Karl Zener of the Parapsychology Laboratory. The twenty-five cards in each pack included five sets, each consisting of five cards with one of the following symbols: star, wavy lines, circle, cross, and square. These simple figures are easy to identify, easy to remember, and have no emotional meaning. By pure chance, without any psi effect, a subject should get a statistical average of 5 hits out of 25 trials.

Adam J. Linzmayer, a student at Duke University, was the first of the outstanding subjects to be studied. In his early tests in 1930, he scored around 5 hits per pack, which was just about average. Then, on May 21, 1931, Linzmayer had a string of 9 consecutive hits. It was the longest succession of correct guesses ever made at Duke—nearly twice as many as pure chance.

Over the next ten days, Linzmayer went through a total of 600 trials. By pure chance, he should have guessed about 120 correctly. Instead, he reached the staggering score of 238 hits—again, about twice as many as by chance only. The odds against getting this high score by chance are more than 10 million to one.

One day, Rhine took Linzmayer for an automobile

ride, to give him some further tests. Rhine had found that many subjects scored higher in relaxed, informal settings. He wanted to see the effect of the auto ride on Linzmayer's already high scores.

Rhine was not disappointed. In going through the 25 cards while seated in the car, Linzmayer scored an amazing 21 hits out of 25. Fifteen were a string of consecutive hits—the longest string ever achieved. The odds of this string of hits by chance alone were many, many billions to one.

But these fantastic runs of success were not to continue. When Linzmayer returned to school after the summer vacation, he seemed to have lost all of his special psi ability. From then on, his scores were always about the chance figures.

Hubert E. Pearce, a divinity student who participated in tests from August 1933 to March 1934, was the highest scorer of all time, and the most famous subject at Duke University. Since G. Gaither Pratt, one of Rhine's assistants, ran the tests, they are now known as the Pearce–Pratt experiments. They are a classic in the field of parapsychology.

In these tests, Pratt was in the Parapsychology Laboratory, which was located in the Duke University Physics Building. For some of the trials Pearce was in the Library, 100 yards away; for the others he was in the Medical Building, 250 yards away. They agreed on the exact times for starting and ending each trial.

Over the months, they ran a total of 1,850 trials in these experiments. Chance would account for an average of 370 hits. Pearce, instead, was correct 558 times. According to Pratt, Pearce's hits were obtained at odds of 10 billion billion to one!

Soon after this remarkable demonstration, Pearce received a letter that contained some very bad news. He never discussed the contents of the letter with anyone, but from then on his scores were within the normal, chance range.

In the many thousands of trials that Rhine and his co-workers ran during the 1930s, on many hundreds of subjects, none came up to the level of Pearce. Many, however, were high scorers who produced results well above the level of pure chance. As a general rule, any results beyond the odds of a hundred to one were considered significant, and worthy of further study.

Almost all of the experiments run in the Parapsychology Laboratory used Zener cards. To test telepathy, the agent selected a card, looked at it, and sent the image to the subject. To test clairvoyance, the agent selected the card, but did not look at it, and asked the subject to try to receive the image from the card itself. To test precognition, the subject named the top card in the pack before the agent shuffled the deck and checked to see the top card.

The Parapsychology Laboratory also did experiments on psychokinesis, the ability to move or change objects by psi forces. Here the tool was either a pair of dice, or a single die. The usual tests were either to try to influence the numbers that showed on the dice, or to cause them to land in a particular area when thrown on a marked table.

Over the long period of research at the Parapsychology Laboratory, Rhine made certain general findings. For one thing, subjects who score high in one branch of psi usually score high in other branches as well. Also, psi abilities seem to have no connection with other factors, such as the age, intelligence, sex, or nationality of the subject. And these abilities are not affected by distance.

Better-than-chance performers have certain characteristics in common. Believers in ESP always score higher than nonbelievers. In Gertrude Schmeidler's well-known experiments at the City University of New York, believers, or "sheep," as she calls them, consistently did better than nonbelievers, or "goats." Also, the outgoing, extroverted personality in a relaxed state always does better than the retiring, introverted individual in a tense state. Psi performance, unlike other learning, does not improve with practice, and does not respond to any system of rewards or punishments. Sooner or later, every high-scoring subject in parapsychology experiments loses his or her high-scoring ability. (Parapsychologists give three possible explanations: boredom, a lack of motivation after demonstrating their ESP, or an inhibition about displaying so rare a gift.) And finally, no subject has ever achieved an absolutely perfect record of hits.

Rhine's research in the 1930s spurred on many other scientists. Samuel George Soal, a mathematics professor at London University and a student of psi, repeated Rhine's experiments. He ran 128,350 trials with 160 subjects from 1934 to 1939. But his results were most disappointing. Not one subject scored above pure chance.

Somewhat later, he reexamined his results to see if

the subjects had "displaced"—named a card that came one or two cards before or after the correct card. Two subjects were found to be displacing and showing psi ability.

Among other American scientists, Professor W. S. Cox, a psychologist at Princeton in 1936, tested 132 subjects with 25,064 trials and reported no evidence of ESP in any one of them. Other researchers at Colgate, Southern Methodist, Brown, and Johns Hopkins universities were also unable to discover any subjects who scored much above chance.

Not only were outside researchers unable to duplicate Dr. Rhine's high scores of the '30s, but Rhine himself no longer uncovered any high scores.

Doubt and suspicion replaced the earlier enthusiasm for parapsychology. Many now wondered: Can parapsychology be considered a science if the same experiments and results cannot be duplicated by other scientists? And, did the high scores disappear because improved experimental methods lessened chances for conscious or unconscious fraud?

Rhine never gave up his belief in the experimental evidence of ESP. Parapsychology, he held, is a very young science, and has not yet reached the point where experiments can be duplicated, as in other sciences. And he was convinced that his test conditions did not allow fraud to affect the results. Rhine and others, however, agreed that there were some areas of weakness in parapsychological research; and that some results might come from factors other than ESP.

Other Explanations of ESP

Some high scores, according to Rhine, might be nothing more than chance or coincidence. A large enough number of trials is bound to give some exceptionally high scores, as well as some exceptionally low scores. Also, he said, the statistics used in parapsychology laboratories might be at fault. Today, though, even the strongest critics of parapsychology agree that most laboratories do use valid statistics.

Rhine considered fraud and cheating as other possible explanations of very high ESP scores. Over the years there have been several proven examples of fraud. Take the case of Smith and Blackburn, for example.

Nearly thirty years after their demonstrations, Blackburn explained how they had fooled the scientists of the SPR. While Blackburn was concentrating on the shapes in the drawing handed to him by an onlooker, he was also making a copy of the drawing on a small piece of cigarette paper that he had hidden in his hand. He tucked the drawing into the clip of a metal pencil which he laid on the table. When Smith later reached his hand out from under the blanket, he grasped the pencil with the cigarette paper drawing. Covered by the blankets, it was then easy for him to remove the blindfold and make a copy of the drawing on a full-sized piece of paper.

Professor C. E. M. Hansel of the University of Wales points out three weaknesses in the Van Damm experiments. First, the observer watching Van Damm also knew which square was being sent. This knowledge might possibly have caused him to mistake the squares that Van Damm chose.

Second, the observer watched Van Damm from the room above and through the two panes of glass in the floor. The glass may have created distortions and caused inaccuracies in his observations. A better place for the observer would have been next to Van Damm.

Third, the experimenters in the room above Van Damm may have consciously or unconsciously given the subject clues by shuffling or tapping. These sounds could easily have been heard by Van Damm.

In the Linzmayer–Rhine tests, Linzmayer scored his biggest success, 15 hits in a row, with a total of 21 hits out of 25, while seated alongside Rhine on the front seat of a car. With the crowded conditions, and the many glass, mirror, and shiny metal surfaces, could he either have seen the cards or reflections of the cards?

In the famous Pearce–Pratt long-distance tests, Pearce was in the Library and Pratt was in the Physics Building. Hansel has shown that it was possible for Pearce to have left the Library, peeked through the glass transom over the door of Pratt's room, seen the list of cards, and gone back to the Library, without anyone in the Parapsychology Laboratory knowing.

These tests are but a few of the many where there is either proof or at least a possibility of cheating.

The third possible explanation that Rhine offered is that the set-up of the parapsychology tests is not as well-designed or as tightly controlled as other scientific experiments. Some parapsychologists explain this as necessary since subjects get better results in relaxed and informal settings, as compared to strict, foolproof laboratory conditions.

Sometimes, Rhine suggested, ESP subjects pick up sensory cues from the agents or from the test materials. For example, the Zener cards that were used in early experiments had all been printed by one company. The pressure used to print the cards was so great that the symbols could be felt if the subject gently rubbed the back of the card. They could also be seen if the light struck the back of the card at a sharp angle. Slight differences in size among the cards of different symbols also made it possible to detect them in that way. Sensory cues, then, may have played a part in tests in which the subjects touched the cards or saw the backs of the cards.

Finally, Rhine said there might be cases in which the subjects obtained high scores by logic and reason. In tests of telepathy or clairvoyance, some subjects may have kept track of the symbols that had appeared on target cards. Then, by knowing which cards had not yet appeared, they could improve their scores as they reached the end of the run.

In tests of psychokinesis that use dice with hollowed-out dots to represent the numbers, the subjects that try to produce higher numbers usually score better over long runs than the subjects that try to produce lower numbers. The reason is that the sides with higher numbers, and more hollowed-out dots, are slightly lighter. They tend to come out on top more often than the lower numbers, which are slightly heavier.

Studies in Parapsychology Today

The science of parapsychology continues to grow despite the number of questions and criticisms of its methods and results. In 1965, Dr. Rhine retired from Duke University, and its Parapsychology Laboratory closed its doors. He went on, though, to organize the Foundation for Research on the Nature of Man. Within this organization he set up the Institute for Parapsychology, in Durham, to carry on research in psychic phenomena.

On December 30, 1969, parapsychology achieved the same status and recognition as the other sciences: the Parapsychology Association was accepted for membership in the American Association for the Advancement of Science.

Important new centers for parapsychological research have sprung up throughout the country. In California there is the Langley-Porter Institute in San Francisco, and the Institute for Noetic Sciences in Palo Alto. The latter was founded by Edgar Mitchell, an astronaut and the sixth person to walk on the moon. In Durham, in addition to the Institute for Parapsychology, we also find the Psychical Research Institute. Another active laboratory is at the Menninger Foundation in Topeka, Kansas.

But perhaps the best-known of the modern parapsychology laboratories is the Division of Parapsychology and Psychophysics in the Maimonides Medical Center in Brooklyn, New York. The leading researcher here is Charles Honorton.

In one set of experiments, the Maimonides researchers are testing the belief that it is easier to receive telepathic messages in a dream state than when awake. The subject is wired up to instruments that measure brain-wave activity and rapid eye movements. He or she goes to sleep in a sealed, sound-proofed room. When the measurements show that the subject is asleep and dreaming, an agent in another room looks at a picture, and sends the image to the dreaming subject. The subject is then awakened and asked to describe his or her dream into a tape recorder.

Another set of experiments tests the theory that ESP improves when all sensory input is removed from the subject. This time, the subject is wide awake in a sound-proofed room. The subject's eyes are covered with two half Ping-Pong balls that diffuse the light, and his or her ears are covered with heavy earphones that block out all sound. While the subject is deprived of all sensory stimuli through both eyes and ears, an agent in another room sends images to the subject by telepathy. The subject describes the picture that is being received.

The Maimonides research has produced some remarkable results. Time after time, the subjects are able to describe pictures sent by the agents. The number of hits is well above chance. These tests, conducted under strict experimental conditions, using automated testing equipment, have renewed a belief in ESP among many scientists who had difficulty in accepting some of the earlier findings.

4

ASTROLOGY

ASTROLOGY: *Using a knowledge of the stars and planets to predict future events on earth.*

The fourteenth-century Italian astrologer Cecco d'Ascoli used the stars to determine the exact time of the birth of Christ. He also calculated the moment of His death on the cross. This was considered blasphemy, and he was burned at the stake in Florence in 1327.

One day in 1470, the French astrologer Pierre le Lorrain observed a comet streak across the sky. This event, he announced, foretold the death of Pope Paul II, head of the Catholic Church, on July 26, 1471. But as the Pope was in perfect health, Pierre was thrown into prison and sentenced to die for blasphemy if his prediction did not come true.

On the afternoon of the announced day, le Lorrain's friends came to his cell to bid him farewell. There seemed little likelihood that he would escape death.

Astrology

But, late that night, the Pope was stricken with an unknown disease that took his life. Le Lorrain was released from prison, and many honors were bestowed on him.

Catherine de Medici (1519–1589), Queen of France, was married to King Henry II. For ten years she was unable to bear a child. Finally, as she was a strong believer in astrology, she consulted an astrologer. After following the astrologer's advice, she became pregnant, and bore a son in 1544.

Much later, the astrologer warned her to "beware of St. Germain." Since her palace was in the St. Germain district of Paris, the Queen moved to another part of the City. On January 5, 1589, she took ill in her new residence. A priest was called in to speak with her. That evening, Catherine died very unexpectedly. The priest's name—Julien de St. Germain!

Evangeline Adams, the first outstanding American astrologer, in 1899 saw a sign in her own horoscope that led her to move from Boston to New York City. She took rooms in the Windsor Hotel, which was owned by Warren F. Leland.

Before moving in, on March 16, 1899, Miss Adams offered to do Leland's horoscope. The chart showed that Leland was facing great danger. The following day, the Windsor Hotel burned to the ground. Several members of Leland's family were killed in the blaze.

In 1914, Evangeline Adams was arrested for being a fortune teller. In court, she defended her practices, and offered to cast a horoscope for a person known only to the judge, as long as he gave her the person's date, hour, and place of birth. With just these clues, Evangeline presented a perfect description of the judge's son. The amazed official waived all charges, and dismissed the case.

The First Astrologers

These are just a few of the many stories on the use of astrology to foretell the future and to read people's character. Astrology, the study of the stars and planets and how they influence life on earth, dates back nearly 3,000 years, to the ancient land of Babylon.

The practice of astrology is linked to the early discoveries of astronomy. The ancients noticed that the changing positions of the sun brought about changes in the season, and that the changing positions of the moon were connected with shifts in the tide. Since the sun and moon have such powerful effects, they reasoned, the other stars and planets also have some sort of influence on events on earth. Astrology, then, was an effort to add meaning to the observations and studies of astronomy. It was not an effort to learn more about the stars and planets.

The early astrologers divided the night sky into twelve sections. Each one was identified by a group of stars known as a constellation. These constellations make up the twelve signs of the Zodiac. The astrological year begins in the spring with the sign of Aries. It then goes through Taurus, Gemini, Cancer, Leo, Virgo, Libra, Scorpio, Sagittarius, Capricorn, Aquarius, and Pisces.

33 Astrology

The idea of the Zodiac was developed and improved over the following centuries. Around the year A.D. 130, Ptolemy, the Greek atronomer and astrologer, wrote *Tetrabiblos*. In this book, he set forth many of the basic ideas of astrology, which are still accepted today.

According to Ptolemy, the sun enters a new sign each month. People born when the sun is in a particular sign are under the influence of that sign. Evangeline Adams described the general characteristics of people born under the different signs this way:

Aries the Ram, March 21 through April 19: Original thinker; keen creative mind. Impractical; if not quickly successful, turns to other work. Must develop patience and ability to stick to task. Very logical, and willing to fight for what seems right. Good in business but works better alone than in group. Often suffers from headaches. Frequent mole or birthmark on face.

Taurus the Bull, April 20 through May 19: Strong and stubborn. Slow to start, but once in motion stays with job until finished, even when little chance of success. Emotions are stronger than reason; if annoyed, quick to anger and rage. Needs to control emotion and temper. Should take time to make decisions and choose course of action. Makes a good friend; kind and generous.

Gemini the Twins, May 20 through June 20: Changes mind quickly and often, depending on whim and mood. Easily learns new skills and sets out on new tasks. Happiest when following two different lines of work at the same time. If concentrating on just one goal, can achieve great success; if not, becomes very depressed. Clever and witty; often becomes an artist, able to see and hear better than most people.

Cancer the Crab, June 21 through July 22: Usually set in ways; prefers the old and traditional over the new and experimental. Strong family ties; loyal to friends and co-workers. Sometimes tries to extend friendship, or even love, to those who turn away. Angry when wronged. Enjoys travel, entertainment, and socializing.

Leo the Lion, July 23 through August 21: Strong and masterful, brave and ambitious. Always ready for a fight, and therefore seldom challenged. Able to inspire and give strength to others. Tends to be lazy and to avoid boring tasks. Too trusting of others; must learn not to believe and accept everything. Makes a good doctor or stage performer.

Virgo the Virgin, August 22 through September 22: Good mind, good memory. Concerned with details; neat and orderly. Tends to be shy; does not always put forth new ideas or suggestions, even though they would be welcome. Self-conscious before an audience. Likes to plan for future; worries more than necessary. Solitary.

Libra the Scales, September 23 through October 22: Balanced and in harmony. Good as a friend. Easily angered by vulgarity or injustice. Depends on intuition; good at judging people and making decisions. Sensitive to feelings of others; can be swayed by arguments or pleas. Often musical. Makes a good business executive.

Scorpio the Scorpion, October 23 through November 21: Bold, confident, and determined. Strong will to succeed. Quiet, modest appearance, coupled with firm resolve. A source of strength to those who tend to be indecisive. Puts off doing unpleasant jobs. Many become outstanding physicians or business leaders.

Sagittarius the Bowman, November 22 through December 21: Active and cheerful, bold and free. Impulsive behavior is catchy; fun to be with. Frank and outspoken; earns respect and honor from others. Needs people's love, and is willing to work hard to earn it. Energetic. Able to concentrate best on only one task at a time; sets very high personal goals.

Capricorn the Goat, December 22 through January 20: Serious and scholarly; good thinker. Able to work hard; shows great self-respect. Steady and trustworthy; strong concern for the future. Enjoys being alone at times; enjoys holding beliefs that are not widely held. Suffers from criticism; does much better work with praise and encouragement.

Aquarius the Water Bearer, January 21 through February 19: Kind and generous; usually quiet and dreamlike in appearance. Feels for others, and willing to make sacrifices to help. Not always practical; makes unreasonable demands on self. Tends to be physically lazy, while very active mentally. Good advisor because of concern for others. Good mechanical skills.

Pisces the Fish, February 20 through March 20: Quiet, modest and calm. Knows more than shows or tells. Often too generous; trusting nature may lead to failure. Jovial; has many friends. Good common sense. Should be firm, and stick to decisions; should not be swayed by others. Enjoys working in group, accomplishes most this way.

How well does the description of your birth sign fit your personality? How well does it work for your friends or members of your family?

Astrology Today

About 32 million men and women in the United States find horoscopes helpful. These believers in astrology buy about two million copies of astrology magazines every month. They read the daily horoscope columns that are found in 1,200 of the 1,500 newspapers published in this country. And they visit and support about ten thousand professional astrologers. Among Evangeline Adams's clients for frequent horoscope readings in the 1920s were J. P. Morgan, the financier; King Edward VII of England; Enrico Caruso, the famous opera singer; and Mary Pickford, the movie star.

In India, couples that are planning to marry usually have a horoscope prepared. The horoscope suggests the best day for the marriage ceremony. It also tells them if their marriage has good prospects.

Professional astrologers prepare horoscopes much more detailed than those that appear in newspapers or magazines. Their horoscopes are drawn up for specific individuals, rather than for large groups of people.

To do your horoscope, the astrologer needs to know the exact time, date, and place of your birth. With this information, he or she consults charts that show the location of the constellations, as well as the position of the sun, moon, and planets at that time. The astrologer notes the heavenly bodies that were entering and leaving the scene, and those that are at their high points. He or she measures the angles between the planets.

After the horoscope is drawn, or "cast," the astrologer interprets the chart. Each horoscope fits only one person—and his or her twin. It is in the shape of a circle. The outside band is divided into twelve equal sections, each one showing the symbol for a different sign of the Zodiac. Within the sections there are divisions, called decans or decantes, of about ten days each. During each decan the positions of the planets—Mars, Venus, Mercury, Jupiter, Saturn—and of the sun and moon are slightly different, and therefore have slightly different meanings.

The astrologers describe a person's traits and characteristics, and future prospects, according to the basic birth sign. Then they add the planetary influence of the person's particular decan, which modifies and tempers the Zodiac reading. The decans are always treated as secondary to the Zodiac.

Most astrologers agree that the interpretation of birth signs and planetary influence is both a science and an art. The science consists of knowing the meanings of the various signs and planets in all their possible combinations. The art consists of being able to apply the messages from the heavenly bodies to individual people.

Although it takes training and experience to cast horoscopes similar to those prepared by professional astrologers, it is possible to prepare a good, simple horoscope based on information already provided in the list of the twelve signs of the Zodiac. One way you can make the information more exact is to pay attention to the cusps, the few days that include the last day of one sign and the first week of the next. People who are born between two signs of the Zodiac are believed to show characteristics of both signs.

Pisces–Aries, March 20 to 27: Adds thought and caution to a drive for action. May later regret impulsive actions.

Aries–Taurus, April 19 to 29: Strives very hard to achieve goals. Should only undertake worthwhile projects.

Taurus–Gemini, May 19 to 26: Shows good blend of quickness and ability to change direction. Good chance of success with concentration and hard thinking.

Gemini–Cancer, June 20 to 27: Practical sense guides busy and active achievers to good, safe projects. Excited by new directions, yet appreciative of old ways.

Cancer–Leo, July 22 to 29: Exuberant and ambitious, self-confident and high-minded. Needs to be careful that good qualities are not overtaken by weakness of character.

Leo–Virgo, August 21 to 28: Combines great enthusiasm with intellectual curiosity and sympathy for others. Will be successful if able to overcome tendency to show off.

Virgo–Libra, September 21 to 29: Improves sense of fairness and good judgment with quickness of mind and ability to analyze problems logically.

Libra–Scorpio, October 21 to 29: Looks for pleasure

and excitement, yet willing to work hard to pursue worthwhile goals. Should avoid tendency to delay making decisions.

Scorpio–Sagittarius, November 20 to 28: Able to succeed at almost all projects, from limited tasks to life-long ambitions. Sometimes sets goals that are too high, and therefore unrealistic.

Sagittarius–Capricorn, December 20 to 28: Learns quickly and well; usually earns excellent marks in school. To avoid despair that comes with failure, needs to avoid overwork and excessive ambition.

Capricorn–Aquarius, January 19 to 26: Understands difficult ideas of math, science, and philosophy, but sometimes troubled by own fears. Should strive to work with others, and avoid being alone.

Aquarius–Pisces, February 18 to 26: Shows great self-understanding and understanding of others. Patiently awaits desired outcomes.

For even greater depth in your horoscopes, you should also consider the planetary influences on your sign and decan. Here is a summary of the influences of each of the planets, plus the sun and moon:

Sun: Strong influences; works mostly on people, less on events. Signifies nobility, sturdiness, and dependability. Can lead to great success, but care must be taken to avoid the temptation of excess.

Moon: Controls destiny by modifying and sometimes weakening the influence of the other planets. Can be overcome by focusing energy on the good aspects of the planetary influence.

Mercury: Strong intellect, which may be used for good or evil. Education very important. Tendency to act rashly and without thought.

Venus: Love, kindness, and sympathy are strong, but they can become false and self-serving. Success is best achieved through peaceful means.

Mars: Power and strength of mind and body. Able to overcome many difficulties. Achieves success through force. Beware of accidents, particularly those caused by metal.

Jupiter: Outgoing, warm-hearted, and giving nature are strongest traits. Adds purpose and dignity when combined with other signs.

Saturn: Wise, with an inner strength. Balances joy and sadness to create outer calm. Dislikes change, and tries to return to the old. Often brings out the faults in other signs.

Below is a list of the twelve signs, and their planetary influences. Under each one are the decans, and their planetary influences:

Aries: Mars
  March 21–30, Mars and Jupiter; March 31–April 9, Sun; April 10–19, Venus and Jupiter.
Taurus: Venus
  April 20–29, Mercury and Mars; April 30–May 9, Moon and Mercury; May 10–19, Saturn.

Gemini: Mercury
   May 20–29, Venus and Jupiter; May 30–June 8, Mars and Venus; June 9–20, Sun and Saturn.

Cancer: Moon
   June 21–July 2, Moon and Venus; July 3–12, Mars and Mercury; July 13–22, Jupiter and Moon.

Leo: Sun
   July 23–August 1, Saturn; August 2–11, Jupiter; August 12–21, Mars.

Virgo: Mercury
   August 22–31, Sun; September 1–10, Venus and Saturn; September 11–22, Saturn and Venus.

Libra: Venus
   September 23–October 2, Moon; October 3–12, Saturn; October 13–22, Mercury and Jupiter.

Scorpio: Mars
   October 23–31, Mars and Venus; November 1–10, Sun and Jupiter; November 11–21, Moon and Venus.

Sagittarius: Jupiter
   November 22–December 1, Mercury; December 2–11, Moon and Mars; December 12–21, Sun and Saturn.

Capricorn: Saturn
   December 22–January 1, Jupiter; January 2–10, Mars and Venus; January 11–20, Mercury and Sun.

Aquarius: Saturn
   January 21–30, Venus; January 31–February 9, Mercury; February 10–19, Venus and Moon.

Pisces: Jupiter
   February 20–29, Saturn; March 1–10, Moon; March 11–20, Mars.

To describe more fully the subject of the horoscope, look up the day of the week of his or her birth. The further planetary influence is said to shade the forces that work on an individual. Some say that this influence dominates the others; some say it just further modifies the total picture.

The ruling body of people born on:
  Sunday is the Sun.
  Monday is the Moon.
  Tuesday is Mars.
  Wednesday is Mercury.
  Thursday is Jupiter.
  Friday is Venus.
  Saturday is Saturn.

Casting a complete horoscope is a long and difficult job. You must know the exact time, date, and place of the subject's birth and have charts that show the positions of the planets at that time. You must be able to work out all the details of the horoscope mathematically. And you must have a thorough knowledge of astrology to interpret the horoscope after it is finished.

You can, however, prepare a simple horoscope. Start with the birth sign of your subject. On a piece of paper, jot down the characteristics that apply to this person. If the subject was born on a cusp, add those characteristics to the others. Make changes in the birth-sign characteristics to include the influence of the cusp.

Finally, add the planetary influences of the birth sign, the decan, and the day of the week. Again go back to the birth-sign characteristics and adjust them for the planetary influences.

Try to discover how accurate your simple horoscope is in describing your subject's character. Do you think the advice in horoscopes can help people to understand themselves better, and help them to plan for the future?

Astrology: Fact or Fiction?

Despite the fact that millions of people today believe in astrology—and that these principles have been accepted for over three thousand years—millions more do not accept astrology at all.

The nonbelievers argue that astrology is at odds with science. If your life is influenced by the stars and planets, they must send out some special vibrations at the moment of your birth. How is this force transmitted from the heavens to earth?

The only forces known to natural science that might have any effect are gravity, magnetism, or some sort of radiation. However, scientists have not been able to detect the slightest effects of any one of these on newborn infants. In fact, they find a greater pull of gravity on the baby from the doctor's body than from any planet. Also, the hospital delivery room effectively screens the newborn infant from any possible effects of radiation.

The believers hold that the planetary influences are transmitted as vibrations that cannot be received or measured by scientific instruments.

Another argument against astrology was stated by St. Augustine back in the fifth century. He cited twin brothers of his acquaintance; one was a wealthy landowner, the other his slave. How could two brothers, born under the same astrological sign, become such completely different kinds of people?

To this question, astrologers answer that the stars lead or incline people in a direction, but they do not force them to go that way. A horoscope, one modern astrologer wrote, is like the listing of TV programs in a newspaper. It gives the names of the shows, but it does not give you every detail of the program content. And there is always the possibility that an unscheduled show will be shown instead of the one listed.

Finally, nonbelievers compare astrology to the magic of correspondence. The constellations and planets were named after the Greek gods who, in ancient times, were believed to have certain characteristics: Taurus, strong and stubborn; Venus, beautiful; Mars, warlike; and so on. Then, by correspondence, the horoscopes ascribe these characteristics to the people born under the particular sign or planet. Hence, someone born under Venus is beautiful, and someone born under Mars is warlike.

The answer given by the astrologers is that, ancient magic or not, millions of people find truth and wisdom in astrology.

These arguments have raged on for centuries. There have been long periods of time when astrology was widely condemned. At other times, like the present, it is widely accepted.

Those who believe in astrology find that it is a helpful guide to living. Those who do not believe in astrology hold that it is dangerous, and that it encourages people to avoid taking responsibility for their actions, and to do things not in their best interests.

Other Ways of Foretelling the Future

Astrology is just one of many methods used to forecast future events. Since the time of ancient Egypt, people have used Tarot cards for fortune telling. There are seventy-eight picture cards, or keys, in the Tarot deck. Twenty-two make up the Major Arcana. These are the ones that are used for readings. They have names such as "Fool," "Lovers," "Devil," "Strength," and "Justice." The other fifty-six cards, the Minor Arcana, are in four suits, similar to the four suits in modern playing cards. The Minor Arcana is not used for readings, but modern cards can be used. Various people have different methods of reading cards, and place varying meanings on all the possible combinations.

The Oriental version of Tarot cards is *I Ching* or *Book of Changes*. This old Chinese text lists sixty-four diagrams made up of combinations of six broken or unbroken lines. Each combination has a special significance. You find your particular combination either by tossing coins or, in a more complex method, by tossing fifty short, narrow sticks.

Similar methods of fortune telling are based on tosses of dice or by reading the leaves left in a cup of tea.

A few forecasting methods are based on body characteristics. Of these, the most frequently used approach is palm reading. Here the lines and folds and shape of the hand give the experienced reader insights into what the future holds. Phrenology achieves the same ends by studying the bumps on the head. Physiognomy examines the facial shape and the lines on the face.

There are some who have developed a skill in interpreting dreams or handwriting. These are both personal and unique; no two people have the same dreams or the same handwriting. Many believe that studying someone's dreams and handwriting can reveal a great deal about the person's character, and furnish clues to his or her future.

5

PSYCHOKINESIS

PSYCHOKINESIS: *The ability to change or move objects by mental power only.*

The performer was billed as a leading psychic, capable of amazing demonstrations of psychic power. Already he had read several people's minds, had copied drawings that he had not seen, and described the contents of the pockets of various members of the audience. Now, he was asking for someone to give him a key which he would bend by mental energy. Several people came forward; he chose a key offered by a woman.

He examined the key for a few moments, and gave it back, asking the woman to hold it by the handle. Gently he slid his fingers back and forth along the length of the key. After a few minutes, he took the key and examined it again. The key had not bent. He continued stroking the key.

Suddenly he shouted, "It's bending, it's bending!" The woman's eyes widened, and she, too, gave a cry when she saw the key sagging as though it were made of rubber. The audience, which had been silent during the demonstration, broke into loud and excited applause.

This performer claims to be gifted with a type of psychic ability called psychokinesis, or PK for short. PK is the power to cause things to change or move by psychic or mental energy alone. Today, most PK demonstrations are given by performers on stage or television shows, or are the subject of research in parapsychology laboratories. Up until about 1950, though, most PK demonstrations were given by mediums, men and women who claim to get their psychic energies from people who have died.

Margery's PK

One of the most successful and mystifying mediums in the early years of this century worked under the name of Margery. Her real name was Mina Crandon. She was the wife of Dr. LeRoi Goddard Crandon, a wealthy, well-known Boston surgeon who taught at the Harvard Medical School. Margery showed an amazing ability to summon such PK wonders as table tilting, rapping, bell ringing, musical-instrument sounding, unexplained appearances of birds in a room, the moving about of furniture, and much more.

Margery discovered her psychic abilities on May 27, 1923, when her husband, a nonbeliever in the occult, tried to reproduce the results of a PK demonstration he had read about. In that demonstration, a psychic was able to tilt a table while resting his hands on the table top. Dr. Crandon, Mina, and four friends sat around a similar table and tried to tilt it by psychic means. Only Margery succeeded in tilting the table.

Word of Margery's accomplishment spread. Friends, acquaintances, even strangers, flocked to the Crandon house to watch her bring about the tilting of the table.

As time went on, she began to give regular demonstrations, called séances. She included other PK occurrences in her séances—cold winds blew, even though every window was shut, hands touched the visitors, even though everyone was holding hands around the table, strange sounds came from different places in the room, even though Margery never left her seat, and small objects and big pieces of furniture moved around, although untouched by human hands.

Margery was a most unlikely psychic. As a well-to-do and respected member of the community, people trusted her because she had no need for personal gain. This helped to convince them that the happenings in her elegant home were true examples of PK.

In April 1924, the Crandons applied for the prize of $2,500 offered by *Scientific American* magazine to anyone who could produce a "visible psychic manifestation." Over the following months Margery held several séances for members of the *Scientific American* committee. The committee included a professor from Harvard, two investigators from the American Society for Psychical Research, and the most famous stage magician of all time, Harry Houdini.

On July 23, 1924, Margery held a séance with

members of the *Scientific American* committee present, including Houdini. Houdini sat on Margery's left.

The lights were turned out. In the complete darkness they heard the voice of Walter, Margery's brother, who had died in a railroad accident in 1911. Walter told them that a megaphone, used to amplify the sound of spirit voices, was floating in the air. No one could see it in the total darkness. "Where shall it go?" Walter asked. Houdini requested that it come to him. A moment later the megaphone landed with a loud noise on the floor next to Houdini.

During the séance, whistles sounded. A bell rang from inside a box. The table tilted. A cold wind blew on the committee members. Several members felt strange hands touching their faces.

Later, the committee members met to discuss the demonstration. One member believed that Margery was a true psychic, and that she had earned the *Scientific American* prize. The others were not sure that she had achieved the effects by occult means. Only Houdini was convinced that Margery was a fraud. And he was able to explain how Margery achieved each of these effects.

Houdini's Explanation

First, Houdini told how he had prepared himself for the evening séance. That morning, he placed a very tight bandage around his right leg, just below the knee. The bandage cut off the circulation of blood from the leg. By evening the leg was swollen and very painful. But more important, it was extremely sensitive to the lightest touch. A feather brushing against his skin was easily felt.

Houdini seated himself next to Margery. In fact, he sat so close that his leg rested next to hers. He noticed that just before the bell sounded inside the box, Margery's left leg moved ever so slightly—but enough to reach a box that was on the floor between her feet. He surmised that she pressed her toes on the lid, which triggered a mechanism to ring the bell.

According to Houdini, the explanation for the table tilting was even easier. Since he felt neither her feet nor her hands move while the table tilted, he decided that she must have raised the table with her head. At one point during the séance, he reached under the table with his free left hand and did indeed feel Margery's head.

The cold wind, he believed, was merely Margery blowing in one direction or another. To the observers in the room it felt like a chill wind. Or, the wind could have been created by something as simple as Margery waving her hand in front of someone's face.

The other PK phenomena took place, Houdini reported, at those times during the séance when Margery thrashed about in her trance and lost touch with the men holding her hands at either side.

It was while her hands were free that Margery reached out and touched others around the table, shook a tambourine, beat on a drum, and strummed on an autoharp. She was also able to place the megaphone on her head like a dunce cap, and then toss it off in Houdini's direction. And it was Dr. Crandon, who was always present, whose voice Margery said was that of her dead brother Walter.

Once Houdini gave a stage performance in which he demonstrated many of Margery's PK occurrences. This convinced many believers that Margery was really a fraud.

But there were others who refused to accept Houdini's conclusions. Perhaps some parts of Margery's PK were accomplished by tricks, they said. But trickery could not explain all of the happenings. Surely some of the things that took place were due to the occult. Also, they believed that Margery was under unusual pressure in front of a committee of skeptics. These believers accept the concept that the occult only works with sympathetic and cooperative observers.

Houdini's demonstration, though, did convince the *Scientific American* committee that Margery had not won the $2,500 prize. In fact, the prize money was never awarded; no medium ever satisfied the committee that he or she truly had occult powers.

Uri Geller's PK

On a popular British radio talk show on Friday morning, February 23, 1973, the host, Jimmy Young, introduced a young Israeli, Uri Geller, to his listening audience. They talked of Geller's experiences with PK and other psychic phenomena.

Geller told of the special powers he had noticed since he was a very young child. By the age of three he knew how much money his mother had won or lost at cards—without being told. He recalled that when he was eight years old, a spoonful of soup spilled on to his lap when the metal grew soft and collapsed. Another time, at the zoo with his mother, he got a powerful feeling that they should leave at once. No sooner were they outside the gates than a lion broke free of its cage.

Geller described how his special psychic abilities enabled him to bend metal objects—such as spoons, forks, nails, and rings—without touching them. He described how he could also start clocks and watches that were broken and had stopped running.

At this point in the Jimmy Young Show, Geller offered to try to bend a key supplied by the show's host. Jimmy Young set a thick, heavy key on the table in front of Geller. Geller placed his hand over the key, and prepared to summon his mental powers to force the key to bend. Speaking into the microphone, he urged the listeners, too, to concentrate their psychic energy on things made of metal, to observe the effect on their silverware and keys.

When Geller removed his hand from the key, the key was bent. As the startled Jimmy Young looked on in amazement, the key continued to bend. The entire radio audience heard Jimmy Young shout, "It's bending right in front of me. I can't believe it!"

Although Geller had accomplished this feat many times before, he seemed just as excited as Young. "Look, look," he cried out in genuine enthusiasm, "look what's happening!"

Presently the producer of the radio program rushed

into the studio with several telephone messages from listeners. Message after message told of silverware, keys, and nails bending in homes all over Great Britain: A woman was stirring a pot of soup when the metal ladle went limp. A girl's gold bracelet buckled and bent on her wrist. A policeman reported that several knives and spoons in his kitchen drawer had developed bends. A jeweler reported that several pieces of new silverware in a tray had bent out of shape. And so on.

While the calls kept coming in, Geller continued his studio demonstrations of PK. He held a metal letter opener in one hand and while he stroked it lightly with the fingers of his other hand, it broke into two pieces.

Geller became a popular guest on talk shows, radio and television, on every continent. He also performed before skeptical committees of scientists at such prestigious institutions as the Stanford Research Institute in Menlo Park, California, and London University, in England.

At a performance in New York City's Town Hall, Geller offered to bend a woman's ring. The woman held the ring in her clenched hand while Geller stood next to her, deep in concentration. From time to time, Geller asked her to open her hand, and he examined the ring. Each time he shook his head and returned it.

After several examinations, Geller gave a triumphant shout. He held up the ring for all to see. It had indeed developed a crack. Within minutes the crack widened, and the ring split into two pieces.

On a recent TV show, Geller was given a watch that had every part intact, but was not running. Using his psychic powers, Geller managed to start the watch. Also, by psychic strength, he moved the hands of a running watch. Another time Geller turned the pointer of a compass, and caused a Geiger counter to start clicking wildly by mental means.

Magicians Explain Geller

The professional organization of magicians, the Society of American Magicians, recently formed an Occult Investigation Committee to study psychic and occult phenomena. Its purpose is to determine how many of these phenomena are really magicians' tricks. Most professional magicians believe that Geller is an extremely able and gifted magician, and that he uses magical tricks to give the impression of psychic powers. But they do not believe that he is a psychic. Without any psychic powers, the professional magicians are able to reproduce all of Geller's so-called psychic demonstrations.

Geller's success, the magicians hold, is partly due to the simplicity of his PK demonstrations. He never uses complicated props or equipment that might break down or be discovered. He also has certain advantages over the usual magicians. By warning the audience that his powers are stronger when everyone believes, he has a ready excuse when his demonstration fails. Also, since everyone knows that psychic powers are not completely dependable, he can blame his failures on the fact that he is a psychic, not a magician.

Geller takes plenty of time to accomplish his PK feats, whereas stage magicians have to produce their results very quickly. He has been known to take up to a half hour to bend a spoon or ring, or to start a stopped watch.

While he performs, Geller keeps moving and talking. According to professional magicians, the activity distracts the audience from his manipulation of the objects. His comments also help to convince the audience that they did witness a PK happening, even if their first impression was different.

Geller has had more success in performing before scientists in controlled laboratory situations than before professional stage magicians. Magicians' skepticism, Geller claims, make it impossible for him to succeed in their presence. But could it be that the magicians are better able than the scientists to spot any trickery?

This handsome young performer takes advantage of any situation that supports his claim to psychic power. On an airplane flight from California to New York, the movie projector jammed, spilling out long lengths of film. Geller apologized to the stewardess, attributing the jam-up to an accidental use of his mental powers. Once in a theatre lobby, ice began to tumble out of a soda machine, and again, a candy machine tossed out extra bars of candy. Each time Geller claimed responsibility.

Many magicians say that this adaptability helps Geller to achieve his most popular psychokinetic effects—bending spoons, forks, knives, keys, nails, and similar metal objects.

According to their description, the first few seconds of a Geller PK demonstration are crucial. After he selects a key from someone in the audience, he may hold the key in his hand as he sits down or walks from one place to another. As he moves, they say, he presses the key hard against something solid, starting the bend. (Try it yourself. See if you can bend an old key by pressing one end against a chair frame or table edge.)

These magicians point out that he sometimes places the key on a table while talking to the audience about something else. He could give the key a further bend as he sets it down. Perhaps he finds a reason to drop his handkerchief on the table. When he picks it up, he bends the key still more.

Professional magicians hypothesize that he slips the end of the key into a slot in his heavy brass belt buckle, and applies leverage to the other end. By such methods, Geller could bend the key long before the audience even expects anything to happen.

Geller could then direct the audience's attention to his psychic efforts to bend the key, while making sure that no one can see that the key is already bent. The audience is attentive and watching as Geller summons all his power to bend the key. After a few minutes, he exposes the bent key. The audience usually applauds wildly.

Some believe that the real source of his energy is in the strength of his hands rather than in any psychic power. We know that during the 1967 Israeli–Arab war, Geller was wounded both in his left hand and right arm. After three weeks in the hospital, he was released, but he continued to do the exercises his doctors gave him to build up the strength in both his hands and arms.

Within a short time, he regained full use of his hands and arms. In fact, he continued developing his strength until he achieved extraordinary power in his hands.

But what of the many metal objects that were reported bent in people's homes during Geller's radio demonstration? There are three explanations. First, in most cases, the objects were probably already bent, but no one had noticed. Second, the object was already weakened from use, and an increase of pressure to test the metal led it to break at that moment. And third, the excitement of having their names and their experiences discussed on the radio led some people to bend the objects themselves.

You can test these explanations. Examine all of the spoons in your drawer at home. How many bent spoons do you find? Next, place all of the keys that belong to you and members of your family on a flat table. How many are bent, so that they rock on the table surface? Two magicians, The Amazing Randi and Karl Fulves, have found that about one out of every ten keys is slightly bent—and had not been noticed before. What about yours?

Many magicians are also skeptical of Geller's display of moving the hands of watches. The trick, they say, is usually done when Geller is first handed the watch. As he takes the watch to look at it, he quickly and deftly pulls out the stem, gives it a turn, and presses it back, in a flash.

Then while he summons up his energy under the watchful eyes of the audience, he does not come near the watch. After ten or fifteen minutes of straining to move the hands from a distance, Geller asks someone to look at the watch. Sure enough, the time has changed.

To start stopped watches, Geller may depend on the fact that many such watches do not work because the oil in the works has become thick and heavy. By just holding these watches, the heat of his hands thins the oil and starts the watch, for a while at least. Sometimes, shaking the watch while it is being handled accomplishes the same thing. In fact, some stopped watches can be prepared by watchmakers to start with only a shake or pressure at one point.

How does Geller move the pointer of a compass? If you do not accept that he is a psychic, then the obvious answer is that he uses a magnet. But he always shows that he does not have a magnet hidden in his hands. Magicians wonder though if Geller could have the magnet in his mouth? Taped on an arm, leg, or somewhere else on his body?

What about the clicking of the Geiger counter? It is a fact that a Geiger counter responds only to radioactivity. Again, magicians point to many places in his clothing where Geller could conceal a radioactive substance to set off the Geiger counter.

It is always fascinating to watch demonstrations of PK. The big question, though, is: Are they skillful magical tricks, or true examples of psychical forces at work?

6

SPIRITUALISM

SPIRITUALISM: *A science, philosophy, and religion, based upon communication between the living and the spirits of those who have died.*

The organ plays softly as a group of men and women take their places in the small church on a quiet Sunday evening. The church looks like a Catholic church or a Protestant church. But it is neither. It is a Spiritualist church.

Like all other Christians, the Spiritualists believe in the hereafter; that a person's soul lives on after his or her physical death on earth. But, unlike Protestants or Catholics, Spiritualists offer proof of life after death by communicating with those who have died or, as they say, passed over into the spirit world.

The organ plays until all the members are seated. The Minister leads the congregation in hymns and prayers to start the service. This is followed by a brief sermon. Next comes the Message Service, when the Minister brings messages from the spirit world to members of the congregation.

The ministers of Spiritualist churches are mediums. A medium is someone who has developed, disciplined, and improved his or her ability to receive messages from those who have passed over and entered the spirit world. Spiritualists hold that everyone is capable of communicating with spirits. But mediums are more sensitive, they say, and have the ability in larger measure than others.

The medium in Spiritualist churches is most often a woman. She works by first establishing contact with the members of the congregation by calling out a greeting to them, and asking them to respond. A spiritual harmony is established among those who are present.

The medium receives some very exact messages, and directs these to specific people. She says, "My spirit guide has a message for somebody named Anne. Is there anyone here named Anne?"

Anne identifies herself, and the medium continues. "The spirit tells me you will soon become ill, and may even enter a hospital. But spirit says not to worry, because you will quickly recover, and feel even better than you do right now."

Then the medium gets a message that is much less clear. "I am getting a message for a gentleman who I can't quite identify. He smokes a lot, either a pipe or cigars. Who am I speaking to?"

The medium looks around the church. One man answers, with some hesitation, that it might be him. The medium stares at the man, and then whispers something over her shoulder, as though she were talking to a spirit. "I'm getting more," she continues. "I see you with a knife, or some sort of cutting tool. Am I speaking to you?"

The man volunteers the information that he smokes, and that he uses various saws and knives in his work as a carpenter.

The medium pauses for a few minutes, a look of deep concentration on her face. She speaks again, more softly than before. "You have just made a big decision."

The carpenter nods his head.

"It was a difficult decision to make. You are still not sure that you made the right choice. Do you know what I am talking about?"

The carpenter again nods his head knowingly.

"Spirit tells me it was wise," the medium continues. "It will work out well. But she warns me to tell you not to change your mind. That is dangerous. Stay with your decision."

The man looks somber and grave as he thinks over what she has said.

The Spiritualist's eyes close as she again prepares to receive another spirit message. This time, though, she clasps her chest, as though in pain and finding it hard to breathe.

She speaks. "I am in contact with a man"—her hand begins to tremble on her chest—"who recently passed over into the spirit world. I feel that it was a sudden heart attack. His name is Jack or Gene; something like that. He wants to talk to his widow. Is she here?"

63 Spiritualism

A middle-aged woman rises to her feet. "My husband, Gene, passed over last month. It was a heart attack."

"Gene tells you to go on the trip you are planning. You will enjoy it. And it will help you to start a new life. Gene wants you to be happy."

The woman looks confused. She protests that she has had no thoughts about going on a trip.

Her answer does not disturb the medium. "I only relay the messages I receive," she replies. "Remember what I say, though. The spirit world does not make mistakes. Most likely you will decide to go on a trip within the next few months. Then, think back to what I am telling you now."

The medium continues to bring messages to people in the church, either from her spirit guide or from the departed loved ones of the church members. Whether clear and detailed or vague and general, whether they concern past events or make future predictions, the church members accept them gratefully.

Some ministers follow the Message Service with an Inspirational Talk. The Inspirational Talk is usually on a general topic related to Spiritualism, and is delivered in the voice of some spirit who has taken over the voice of the medium. The pitch, the accent, the use of words, and the facial expression all seem to belong to another person.

The service ends with some more prayers and the singing of hymns.

64 Spiritualism

Services similar to this one are conducted in the two thousand member churches of the National Spiritualist Association of Churches. This organization trains people to become ministers and mediums, and oversees the rules and regulations that govern their activities. The Association also works to keep out those who would use Spiritualist churches for commercial or entertainment purposes. The Association was formed in 1893, just fifty years after the very strange occurrence that marked the birth of modern Spiritualism.

The Fox Sisters

During the night of March 31, 1848, two young girls, Margaret and Kate Fox, living in a small farm cabin in the town of Hydesville, New York, woke their parents. They were frightened and crying, and complained of loud taps and knocks that seemed to be coming from the walls of their attic room.

Mr. Fox searched the room for the source of the sound. He found nothing. He shook the windows to see if the rattle could be coming from there. Amazingly, every time he shook the windows he heard the same number of raps, as though something or someone were answering him.

Just then, Margaret, the older sister, called out, "Here, Mr. Splitfoot, do as I do." (Splitfoot is another name for the Devil, who is reputed to have a cloven, or split, hoof.) And she loudly snapped her fingers. To the terror of the entire family, the spirit rapped back in the exact same pattern!

65 Spiritualism

Mrs. Fox, a devout Methodist, was convinced that it was the Devil rapping, and wanted nothing more to do with it. But Margaret and Kate worked out a way to communicate with the spirit. They devised a code of raps for the spirit to use to answer their questions. One rap meant "no"; three raps meant "yes." By carrying on a conversation in this way, they learned that the raps were being produced by the spirit of Charles B. Rosma, a peddler, who had been murdered in the girls' room and was buried in the cellar of the house.

Word of the strange happening in the Fox cottage spread throughout the area. Large crowds appeared to hear the rappings, to put questions to the peddler's spirit, and to receive answers from the spirit world.

The Fox family moved to Rochester, New York, to get away from the crowds and from the house. But the rapping went with them. Margaret and Kate were able to summon the spirit at will.

Crowds were still attracted to the Fox sisters in Rochester. So Leah, their older sister, rented a public auditorium there, Corinthian Hall, and the girls put on the first public demonstration of spirit communication on November 14, 1849.

The event was immensely successful. Every seat was sold at the then high price of one dollar each. A committee of leading citizens who carefully watched the proceedings pronounced them free of trickery or fraud, a true communication with the spirit world.

Led by their ambitious sister, Leah, Margaret and Kate gave public exhibitions and private demonstrations of their amazing feat. They attracted worldwide attention, and earned vast sums of money.

The first hint of trouble came when three doctors from the University of Buffalo were allowed to hold the sisters' arms and legs during a demonstration. They reported that the raps came only when they were not holding the girls' legs. Therefore, they suggested, the raps were produced by the girls cracking their knee or toe joints, just as people crack their finger knuckles.

Far from driving people away from the Fox sisters, the doctors' report attracted even more interest in the rappings. It started also a new interest in ghosts. Stories of haunted houses and of mischievous ghosts were widely reported. While a good number of people believed in ghosts, there was a general skepticism. Most ghostly incidents were dismissed as the result of either natural causes, delusions, or hoaxes.

For the next forty years large numbers of people believed that the raps came from the spirit world. Moreover, the success of the Fox sisters inspired others to become mediums. Some communicated with rappings, as did Margaret and Kate. But others received messages through trumpets that were suspended in midair, or by seeing writing appear on blank slates. A few mediums produced hands or heads, or even complete bodies, called ectoplasm, that came from the spirit world. They produced flowers, animals, cold winds, and auras of light, among many other effects.

The mediums claimed they could fly through the air, make tables rise while resting their hands on the surface, and cause chairs and other pieces of furniture to move, fall over, and fly about in strange and unexplained movements. They made bells ring and musical instruments sound—even though no one was playing them. To prevent any trickery, the medium would often be tied in his or her chair during these happenings.

The widespread interest in communications from the spirit world did not bring the Fox sisters much personal satisfaction. Both girls had unhappy marriages, and led miserable personal lives. By 1888, they were both heavy drinkers, and destitute. They decided to reveal the secret of the rappings which had unleashed the flood of mediums and the belief in Spiritualism throughout the world.

First, in September 1888, Margaret gave an interview to a reporter from the New York *Herald*. She told him how she and Kate had produced the first raps, back in Hydesville, by tying a string to an apple and bouncing it on the floor and throwing it against the wall. Then, she told how they had learned to make the same noises by snapping their big toes against the wooden footboards of their beds. The wood helped to amplify the sounds, which were quite loud already.

At the end of the interview, the reporter, in disbelief, asked if all the rappings and communications with spirits were a trick. "Absolutely!" Margaret replied. Then she gazed off into space, and asked, "Spirits, is he not easily fooled?" And very loudly and very clearly came three raps, the code signal from Hydesville which meant "yes."

A few weeks later, Kate Fox made a statement to the press. She said, "Spiritualism is a humbug from beginning to end. It is the greatest humbug of the century."

On October 21, 1888, Margaret Fox appeared on the stage of the Academy of Music in New York City. She explained that she and Kate began the rappings as a childish lark and, once started, were afraid to stop. Then she took her shoes off and stepped onto a low wooden platform. She started the rappings, which seemed to come from all over the theatre. Three doctors observed Margaret. They agreed that the sounds were made by the cracking of the first joints of her big toes.

At first there was a stunned silence in the hall. Then bedlam broke loose. People hissed and booed. They could not accept what Margaret had just told them and showed them. "The Church made her do it," said some. "The confession is being paid for by newspapers looking for a story," said others. "She is really a medium without knowing it," said still others.

Now stage magicians came forward and showed how other mediums used hidden props, clever lighting, unseen assistants, and very skillful magical tricks to cause the mysterious effects. Hidden threads and wires worked very well in the darkness where mediums held their seances. Many different props could easily be hidden under their large dresses, in their mouths, or even in their armpits. By preparing the room in advance, the medium could operate pieces of equipment with the slightest movement of a foot, leg, hand or arm.

But still believers in Spiritualism at that time held on to their belief in communication with the other world. In fact, their beliefs grew even stronger. Communication with the spirit world had grown into more than a stage entertainment. It had become a religion.

Andrew Jackson Davis

More than any other single person, Andrew Jackson Davis (1826–1910), is responsible for creating a religion based on communication with the spirit world. Known as the Poughkeepsie Seer, after the small town in New York in which he lived, Davis had always claimed to hear voices from the spirit world. He had studied mesmerism, a type of hypnosis. And he had visions of speaking with some of the great philosophers of the past. From these experiences, he evolved a body of beliefs and ideas which became the foundation for the religion of Spiritualism.

In 1847 Davis received a message that the time of Spiritualism had come. The rappings of the Fox sisters, just one year later, fulfilled this prophecy. Thus, the theories and writings of Davis, together with the proofs furnished by the Fox sisters, mark the beginning of Spiritualism as a religion.

Arthur Ford

Spiritualism grew rapidly until the year 1900. Then, for the next fifty years or so, interest fell off considerably. Many people were disillusioned by tales of trickery and fake. There was little growth in the Spiritualist Church from 1900 to 1950.

Nevertheless, during this period there were some outstanding Spiritualists and mediums. Perhaps the best known was Arthur Ford (1897–1971), who started his career as an ordained minister at the Christian Church in Barboursville, Kentucky, in 1922. Even then he was interested in the occult. He lectured on unexplained mysteries, and on magical practices dating back to the time of the Bible. And he presented public demonstrations of mind reading.

In time, he devoted himself to spirit contacts and mediumship, becoming Minister of the First Spiritualist Church in New York City. It was here, around 1929, that Ford became accepted as one of the leading Spiritualists of the time.

The event that catapulted him to fame was the $10,000 reward offered by the widow of Harry Houdini, famed stage magician, to any medium who brought her a coded message from her dead husband. Up until his death in 1926, Houdini had devoted himself to exposing the fakes and frauds among mediums and psychics. Before he died he promised his wife that if it was possible to communicate from the dead, he would find the way to reach her. He gave her the code that he would use.

For two years, Bess Houdini attended numerous séances and sought out mediums who promised to bring her word from her husband. None gave her a message in the right code. Then, when she was seriously ill with the flu and experiencing periods of delirium, Arthur Ford stepped forward with a carefully coded message from Houdini. The sick, weak woman was convinced that the message was indeed from her dead Harry.

But there were many others who were not as convinced as Bess Houdini. Many questioned whether the woman was of sound enough mind at the time to have known whether Ford had the right code or not. And whether, in her delirium, she had not given the code away to a nurse, who had given or sold the information to Ford.

Others suspected that Harry Houdini had also shared the code with a magician-friend, Daisy White, and that it was she who had furnished Ford with the information. One newspaper writer reported that Ford had admitted that the message had come not from Houdini's spirit but in a much simpler way. Of course, Ford later denied the allegation. But Bess Houdini became very skeptical, and stated on more than one occasion that Arthur Ford had not brought the correct coded message from Harry Houdini, after all.

Arthur Ford and Bishop Pike

By 1966 this controversy had died down, but an even greater one was created when Bishop James A. Pike asked Arthur Ford to help him communicate with his dead son, Jim. The messages that Arthur Ford brought from Jim's spirit contained information known only to the Bishop and his son.

Bishop Pike promoted Arthur Ford's mediumship. They appeared together on a television show where Ford went into a trance and brought Bishop Pike more messages. Millions watched and were struck by Ford's apparent success. On the basis of this publicized incident, many more people became believers in Spiritualism.

Several years later, in 1973, two years after Ford's death, two researchers went through the dead medium's papers. While looking for material for his biography, they came across an immense file of obituaries of well-known and less well known people. There were long lists of people who had made appointments for séances, and of people Ford thought might be making appointments. Next to each name was extensive biographical information collected from many sources.

A secretary who had worked for Ford told how he helped Ford research the background of each of these people. Among Ford's papers were newspaper and magazine articles on Bishop Pike and his son. It is quite possible that Ford expected the Bishop to call on him, and was ready when he finally did.

Developing an Ability as a Medium

Most mediums in the Spiritualist Church became interested in Spiritualism after an experience that they took to be a signal of their ability to receive messages from the spirit world. To develop this ability further, they took instruction from experienced mediums.

The most popular method involves forming a demonstration class or a home circle. Usually these classes or circles are run by trained leaders. They are sometimes conducted by members of the group themselves in an effort to develop their abilities together.

In her book *How to Develop Your ESP*, Suzy Smith

includes Arthur Ford's description of a typical class or circle. It has between four and fifteen members. It meets once a week, at the same time and same place, where there is no danger of being disturbed. Each member is either a believer in Spiritualism, or approaches the subject with an open mind. Curiosity seekers or skeptics, he found, interfere with the progress of all. Also, the members agree to attend regularly and over a long period of time. One-time visitors, and people with irregular attendance as well, spoil it for the others.

As the members of the group arrive at the meeting place, they quietly take their places in a circle. When everyone is assembled, the lights are dimmed, and the group sings a few hymns to set the mood for what follows.

For the next half hour, each person meditates in silence. The mind is open to any messages that might enter. When Reverend Ford guided a class, the members were asked to wear loose clothing and to sit in straight chairs, which he found helped to open the mind. They were asked to block out all external images by thinking of pulling down a window shade in front of their eyes. One of the common experiences is a feeling of "changing your chemicals," as new sensations come to various parts of the body during the meditation period.

After the half hour, the members recount any experiences or messages that they received during that time. The professional medium, if present, tries to explain the occurrences, and to suggest ways to intensify the experience.

At the end of the meeting there are refreshments. The

group also plays games to test and to develop the psychic powers of the members. In one popular game, the members pass around some object—a key, a ring, a scarf—that belongs to a member of the group. Each person, in turn, holds the object and tells the others the thoughts and ideas that the object brings to mind. Later, these remarks are judged to see how well they describe the owner of the object.

Many people around the world are strong believers in Spiritualism. They have a sincere, religious faith that they are witnesses to messages coming to the living from the souls of those who have left the earth plane and entered the spirit world.

There are also many who are convinced that Spiritualism is a fraud and a delusion. They do not accept the possibility of contact between the living and the dead. Among them are the stage magicians who are able to expose many of the tricks used by fake mediums to fool those who have faith in Spiritualism.

And there are psychologists who explain much of what the mediums say and do as the working of the unconscious in mediums and listeners alike. Harry Houdini, the famous magician and exposer of fake psychics, summarized the position of these magicians and psychologists by saying: "Anyone can talk to the dead—but the dead do not answer."

FAITH HEALING

FAITH HEALING: *Restoring good health and relieving pain by nonmedical means, usually based on the flow of psychic energy from healer to patient.*

For years, doctors had been treating a sixteen-year-old girl for cerebral palsy. They had fitted her legs with metal braces to help her walk. They had operated to try to relax her left arm, which was fixed rigidly against her chest. Still, the girl could hardly walk or move her arm, and her fingers were locked in a tight fist.

Disappointed in the results achieved by traditional medicine, her mother brought the badly crippled girl to Ethel de Loach, of Morristown, New Jersey. Mrs. de Loach, a slight, gray-haired woman, is a faith healer. Over the years she found she was able to cure and heal without using any of the methods of modern medicine.

The girl lay down on a sofa in her room, and Mrs. de Loach stood alongside. The Spiritualist closed her eyes, and soon looked serene and peaceful. Still standing in one place, she began to rock back and forth. Her hands moved through the air above the girl's body. At first they moved slowly; then faster and faster. They darted down, lightly touching her deformed left arm. Like weightless birds, Mrs. de Loach's hands flew over the girl, flitting here, flitting there, alighting for a second, then lifting up, gliding along, and swooping down again.

After several minutes, her movements stopped. She dropped her hands to her sides. Her entire body seemed to shrink. With a shake she opened her eyes, like one who has just awakened from a vivid dream.

Mrs. de Loach and an assistant helped the girl rise up from the sofa. For the first time in her life, the young woman was able to move her left arm. She opened her fist and stared at her open hand. A few moments later, she took a step.

After a few more treatments, the girl regained much of the use of her arms and hands.

Royal Festival Hall in London, England, was nearly filled with enthusiastic supporters who had come to see Harry Edwards, best known of the English faith healers in the 1960s, hold a public healing session.

The session opened with several musical selections by the choir. These were followed by some inspirational talks. Finally, Harry Edwards, a heavy, elderly gentleman with a warm, kindly air about him, came out onto the stage.

Edwards told the crowd about some of his cures. Then, he invited all those who wanted to be healed to come up to the stage.

Faith Healing

From all parts of the large hall, crippled and lame, bandaged, trembling, shuffling, and stooped-over people started to make their way to the stage. Those in wheel chairs or on stretchers were carried forward.

Mr. Edwards walked from one to the other. He learned the nature of each person's problem, whether or not there was pain, and how long the illness had persisted. Gently, but firmly, he placed his hand over the trouble spot. For the woman who was bent over with arthritis, he placed both hands on her back. For another, who could not move her right arm, he rested one hand on her shoulder. For the man suffering with asthma, Mr. Edwards placed one hand around his neck and the other over the man's mouth and nose.

The three thousand people in the hall followed closely in complete silence as Mr. Edwards laid his hands on person after person. From time to time they saw his hands shudder as though powerful waves of energy were flowing from him into the diseased part of the patient.

When he removed his hands from the patient, a murmur went through the audience. The woman who had been bent over for five years straightened and stood upright. The other woman, whose arm had been paralyzed, was able to raise her arm to shoulder height. The man with asthma breathed deeply.

The waiting room of the second-floor clinic in Manila, the Philippines, was crowded with fifteen men and women, seated and standing around the room. Every two or three minutes, an assistant came from the inner

78 Faith Healing

room to call the next patient into the operating room. The surgeon was Antonio Agpaoa, the most famous psychic surgeon.

The operating room did not look like a typical hospital room. Instead it was a bare room with a plain wooden table in the center, covered by a sheet. Nor did Agpaoa, or "Dr. Tony" as he is called, look like a typical surgeon. Instead of hospital gown and mask, Agpaoa was dressed in a short-sleeved sport shirt and a pair of slacks.

The patient was there for treatment of her stomach disorder. "Dr. Tony" told her she needed an abdominal operation. He prepared to perform the surgery.

The woman lay down on the table. She was not given an anesthetic or sedative, since this healer's operations are painless.

With his bare hands, Agpaoa started to manipulate the woman's abdomen. He pushed here and pulled there, kneading and tugging at the flesh. The woman showed no signs of pain or discomfort.

Then Agpaoa raised his right hand and brought the side of the hand down sharply on her abdomen. A burst of blood spurted up, splattering "Dr. Tony" and his two assistants. Still the patient showed no sign of pain.

Still using only his bare hands, Agpaoa appeared to reach deep into the wound. In a few seconds he lifted up his hand. He was holding a bloody piece of tissue the size of a peach. He showed the woman that he was placing the diseased tissue from her abdomen into a jar for further study.

Then he explained how he was closing up the cut and using some alcohol to clean the wound. When he was finished, there was no scar. The patient did not feel weak. She got off the table and walked away without help.

Almost everyone has read these stories, or similar ones, in newspapers or magazines. Many have witnessed faith healing demonstrations in person, or have watched them on television. The cures of faith healing are widely reported and widely accepted. Large numbers of people feel that faith healing is able to work in many cases where traditional medicine has failed.

Faith healing is as old as humanity. Most primitive people had their medicine men and shamans who could cure by magic, charms, spells, and other supernatural powers. In the Bible there are accounts of at least twenty nonmedical cures by Jesus Christ. It is said that Jesus was able to cure by touching the sick, called "laying on hands," by prayer, or by simply commanding the person to be well. Among other cures, He was able to stop bleeding, cure fever, restore sight to the blind, restore hearing to the deaf, and restore motion to the paralyzed.

Faith healing is particularly widespread in England. A recent poll showed that four out of five people there believe in faith healing and psychic surgery. Harry Edwards is a good example of the popularity—and success—of faith healing. He attributes his success to the spirits of two dead scientists, Louis Pasteur and Joseph Lister. They enter his body, he says, and give him the psychic energy to cure and heal. By his own estimates, he treats over two thousand people a year. Of these, he claims that he improves the condition of between 80 and 90 percent, and that he cures between 30 and 40 percent.

Medical Doctors Appraise Faith Healers

According to medical doctors, faith healers are successful in certain cases only. They often take credit for cures of illnesses which would have disappeared with or without their help. They may also help those who suffer from psychosomatic illnesses, those that are caused by mental, rather than physical problems. Among the illnesses that might be psychosomatic in origin are headaches, indigestion, ulcers, asthma, skin disease, and even blindness, deafness, or loss of speech. If there is no organic or physical cause for the symptoms of disease, the faith healer can sometimes help the symptoms to disappear.

Doctors also believe that the excellent success records of some faith healers come from patients who are convinced that they feel better, even though they really are still sick. And finally, faith healers show great success with the fakes—those who pretend to be sick, so that they can then appear to be cured and enjoy the publicity that ensues.

Members of the medical profession insist that in most cases the faith healers accomplish nothing. If anything, the doctors say, they harm the patients by delaying treatment by trained physicians.

Dr. Louis Rose, a British psychiatrist, studies faith

81 Faith Healing

healing. He tells of a public demonstration in which Harry Edwards cured a lame woman so that she was able to walk back to her seat without any help. Later, though, Dr. Rose saw the same woman in the street, and she was able to walk only with the use of two canes.

Investigators are not able to check the accounts of most faith healers. The healers keep very poor records. They do not record the patient's condition either before or after the faith healing experience.

Also, many faith healers, such as Harry Edwards, suggest that their patients go for regular medical help at the same time as they receive faith help. They want to avoid the criticism that faith healing delays treatment by a medically trained physician in cases which cannot be cured by faith healing. Combined treatment, however, makes it difficult to discern how much the patient is affected by the faith healer, and how much by the physician.

Dr. Rose recently completed an in-depth study of ninety-five faith-healing cases. Of this group, fifty-eight people had no medical records, and there was no way to measure the effect of the faith healing. In twenty-two cases, the before and after medical records differed substantially from the accounts told by the patients or their faith healers; these cases were not studied further.

Fourteen people showed improvement. Of these, three maintained their healthier condition; three later relapsed to their original condition; four people felt better, but did not show any physical or organic change upon medical examination; and four received medical treatment at the same time, making it impossible to measure the role of the faith healing. The condition of only one patient actually worsened.

This study, and others, on faith healing seem to show that faith healing works more often than not. These cures, however, are not "miracle" cures. Rather they are cures that are helped by the power of suggestion. The chief danger, and it is a very important one, is that people will rely on faith healing alone and neglect regular medical care.

Psychosurgery is one type of faith healing that magicians are able to duplicate. The magician pinches a fold of skin, as the psychic surgeon did to form a crease that looks like a cut. The squirting blood is squeezed out of a sponge or soft plastic container hidden in the palm of the hand. The tissue that is removed during the magician's "operation" could be an animal organ that was also hidden by the surgeon or an assistant, a part of a pig's intestine passed off as the cancer, tumor, or ulcer. Of course, in these "operations" there is no scar, since there is no cut.

Faith healing involves millions of people today. The most famous healers appear on television shows and in large auditoriums from coast to coast. A number are connected with those churches where healing is part of the service.

On the other hand, most medical doctors and many others deny the value of psychic healing. What is needed are more objective studies on faith healing and more medical research to gain new insights into healing processes in the human body.

8

WITCHCRAFT

WITCHCRAFT: *The practice of magic, for good or evil ends, by witches.*

Early every Saturday evening cars begin to arrive at an ordinary-looking suburban house. The people that walk up the steps and enter the house also look quite ordinary. They include a policeman, a teacher, a salesman, a bookkeeper, and a homemaker, among others.

Inside the house, all seems quite ordinary, too. Except that the arriving people do not get together in the living room or walk into the dining room or kitchen. They head down the stairs to the basement.

Here the scene is anything but ordinary. The basement walls, ceiling, and floor are painted black. The only light comes from the black candles placed about the room. These candles give off smoke and a strong odor. The room is murky and smelly.

Drawings of various geometrical shapes hang on the walls, with strange-looking writing and figures that look like ancient Egyptian tomb decorations. A large eye is painted prominently on one wall. And on another is a large picture of a hairy man, black in color, with horns, cloven feet, and a tail.

The six men and six women who are meeting at this place with their leader are witches. Their group of thirteen (this number was chosen because there are thirteen moons in a year), which conducts the ceremonies and rites of the group, is called a coven. The actual ceremony is called an esbat.

When the entire group is assembled, most of its members take off their clothes. The witches call this being Skyclad. It helps them to summon and transmit the energies they need for their work. A few of the members do not undress.

The leader, or priest, is called the Horned God. If the leader is a woman she is called priestess or Mother Goddess. The Horned God of this coven wears a black mask and a full red satin cape. All of the witches wear many necklaces, rings, and earrings of silver, the moon metal.

One by one the witches step into a circle, nine feet in diameter, drawn with white chalk on the black floor. Inside the circle is a table covered with a black cloth and six burning black candles. Also on the table is an ornate silver wine goblet, or "chalice," a sword, a small knife, several lengths of cord, and a number of stone and silver carvings.

When everyone is inside the circle, the Horned God uses the sword to trace around the chalk line. This ritual, Casting the Circle, is to draw a magic circle around the coven and protect the members from evil. The leader is careful to trace the circle in a counterclockwise direction to add to its power.

One member loudly rings a bell to summon the spirits. The coven then repeats several chants. They invoke the many names of the Devil—Satan, Lucifer, Belial, Karnayna, Balin, and others. They pray for power and wisdom. One prayer, "Eko, Eko, Azarak; Eko, Eko, Aradia," is used to raise the Cone of Power. The Cone of Power is the collective psychic energy of the entire coven, which is pictured as an inverted cone over the magic circle.

The old idea of the Cone of Power is related to the modern interest in pyramids. Pyramids are supposed to be able to focus or concentrate energy on anything or anyone placed within them. People who use pyramids today claim they are able to sharpen dull razor blades, change milk to yogurt, prevent meat from decaying, and increase the owner's psychic energy.

After raising the Cone of Power, the witches join hands and do a snakelike dance inside the circle. The priest either leads the line, or follows at the end. From this ritual comes the expression "The Devil take the hindmost." There are then more prayers and chants before the drinking of the wine from the chalice.

In the next part of the service, the witches report on their most recent magical experiences. Most of today's magic is so-called White Magic—attempts to heal the sick, bring good fortune to those in trouble, solve problems, attract lovers, make friends, secure jobs, and earn money. The priest and other witches suggest ways to increase each member's success with magic. Although there are still some covens that practice Black Magic, they are rare. Black Magic is concerned with spells and curses, bringing bad fortune to one's enemies, causing disease, and even murdering foes.

Then they attempt to summon help to work new magic. A member calls for help to regain the love of his girlfriend; another wants to know whether or not to take a new job; still another needs courage to confront someone who has hurt his feelings.

The particular spells and magic procedures that are conjured up are taken from special books called grimoires. The most famous grimoire is *The Greater Key of Solomon the King*, said to have been written by King Solomon. Each coven adapts parts of one or more grimoires to its own use. A witch that is taken into the coven copies over these particular rituals and rites and spells in his or her own *Book of Shadows*. This is how the traditions of witchcraft, though differing from coven to coven, are passed on through the years.

Following the magic part of the ceremony, many covens initiate new members. Among the more popular rituals is the ceremony of the hands. The priest or priestess of the coven places one hand on the top of the head and one on the soles of the feet of the new member, and dedicates the entire body of the man or woman to the coven.

Often, a small scratch is made on the skin of the initiate, the Mark of the Devil. (During witch hunts, the Mark of the Devil was taken as proof that the accused was a witch. Untold numbers of people died because warts, moles, and scars were judged to be Devil's

Marks.) The Signing in Blood may conclude the initiation. The initiate, the priest, and other members of the coven cut their arms and make blood marks on a piece of parchment to confirm the newcomer as member of the coven.

The concluding part of the esbat is usually festive. There is dancing, drinking, and eating. Though a few covens may end their esbats with a sexual orgy, most covens do not accept this as part of modern witchcraft practice.

Ingredients of Witchcraft

Anton LaVey is High Priest of the Church of Satan, which is based in San Francisco. He believes that to work magic the witch must have a purpose and a strong desire for the end result. Magic should not be used to show off or to entertain others.

Then, the witch must achieve a balance between what he or she desires, and knowledge of what changes magic can effect. Witches cannot move buildings, turn tone-deaf people into opera singers, or make a million dollars appear.

Finally, for the magic to be successful, the witch needs to follow the directions very exactly.

All witchcraft magic uses imagery. Imagery is based on some article or thing associated with the person or event that you want to change. It may be a photo or drawing, some writing, a lock of hair, a fingernail clipping, or an article of clothing. One of the oldest and most powerful objects used in witchcraft is a wax or clay figure of the person on whom the magic is to be worked. These objects help to focus the magical powers.

When using a figure for Black Magic, the witches push pins into it, break off its arms or legs, or throw it into a fire in order to harm the person it represents. A pin stuck into the stomach of the figure, it is believed, will cause the person a stomachache, as well.

In the same way, the witches use figures to heal in a White Magic rite. The witches concentrate on the figure that resembles the sick person, and on the diseased part. They focus on changing the mental image until they feel that they have gotten rid of the sickness. Then they aim the healthy image at the target person—hopefully returning him or her to good health.

Magic used by modern witches to harm their enemies or heal their friends is simple compared to the older magic. A thirteenth-century grimoire instructs witches who wish to foretell the future to catch a weasel and tear out and eat its still-beating heart. A more modern grimoire from the year 1820 states that to win at cards one should tie the heart of a bat to the right arm with a string of red silk.

The idea that witches can fly is one of the most common beliefs of witchcraft. The popular image of a witch shows her flying through the air on a broomstick. Actually, the idea probably arose from rites in which the witch rides a rod or wand like a hobby horse around and around the magic circle.

Also, witches who wish to fly have been known to rub a certain ointment on their skin. The ointment is a mixture of water, hemlock, aconite, belladonna, soot, and fat. Hemlock and aconite are poisons; belladonna, a powerful heart stimulant. All of these ingredients may be absorbed through cracks in the skin. Together they produce mental confusion, dizziness, shortness of breath, and a wild, irregular heartbeat—symptoms not unlike the sensation of flying or falling through space.

Of all the tales about witches, among the most striking are those that tell of witches who are able to turn themselves into animals. France in the sixteenth century was a center of belief in lycanthropy, where witches who were human by day became werewolves at night, attacking and killing people they knew.

In one legend, a hunter returning home late one evening was attacked by a large wolf. The hunter fired his gun at the wolf, but the bullets did not stop the animal. So the hunter drew his knife, and in the struggle managed to cut off one of the wolf's paws. The wolf ran off. The hunter put the severed paw in his sack and continued home.

On the way, he met his closest friend. He wanted to show him the paw. So he reached into his bag and pulled out—instead of the paw—a woman's hand, with a ring on one of the fingers.

One look at the hand and the ring, and his friend turned and ran home. He found his wife sitting near the fireplace, her hands in her lap, hidden beneath her apron. He flung the apron away and discovered that his wife's hand was missing. All that was left was a still-bloody stump.

Angrily he accused her of being a witch and a werewolf. She was found guilty, and was later burned at the stake.

History of Witchcraft

Witchcraft dates back to the time of the earliest people. Witches were part of prehistory and of various pagan cults.

Up until the end of the Middle Ages, witchcraft was considered a carry-over of the pagan world. It was called the Old Religion. Witchcraft and Christianity coexisted.

But then the Christian Church changed its view. It came to consider witches the enemies of the Church. Lurid stories of the witches' Black Mass spread. Tales were told of witches who cursed God instead of praising Him, and prayed to the Devil instead of to Jesus Christ. These accounts told of sexual orgies that were part of the Black Mass. People had their faith in the Christian Church strengthened by hearing stories of being seized by the Devil and dragged off to Hell, as well as by hearing descriptions of the Black Mass.

Witches were accused of having made a pact with the Devil. They were thought to have entered into these pacts in order to do evil deeds by magical means. And they were usually pictured as old, ugly hags, bent over, and twisted with age.

Thus began a period of over four hundred years during which time great numbers of innocent men and women were jailed, tortured, and eventually hanged or burned to death. There are no accurate numbers available, but estimates vary from many thousands up to ten million.

The first recorded witch burning was of Angèle de Labarthe in Toulouse, France, in the year 1275. It was the beginning of the witch-hunting craze that grew in intensity and numbers until it reached a climax at the Salem witch trials in 1692.

In that year about 150 Salem men and women were accused of being witches. Nineteen were hanged and one was crushed to death before the craze passed.

How did Church and civil authorities determine the guilt or innocence of people accused of being witches? One method they used is called pricking. The questioner looked for Devil's Marks on the accused one's body. Any wart, sty, scar, mole, freckle might be a Devil's Mark. A needle was plunged into the mark while the accused was distracted. If he or she did not feel the needle or did not bleed, this was accepted as proof of the presence of a Devil's Mark, and the person was found guilty of being a witch.

Another test involved the ability to float in water. If the accused floated, this was considered proof of guilt. The explanation was that a person floats because his or her soul has been stolen by the Devil. If the accused sank this was proof of innocence. All too often, though, the accused drowned before being brought to the surface and declared not guilty.

Torture was the most popular method of arriving at judgments at witch trials, since a confession was considered the best way to determine guilt. The case of an accused witch in Poland in 1629 shows some of the methods that were used. The woman was bound, her hair cut, and alcohol was thrown over her head and set on fire. Then she was hauled up to the ceiling and left hanging by her arms for three hours. Next, alcohol was thrown over her back and burned. Again she hung by her arms, this time with heavy weights tied to her feet. Later she was flogged with a whip, and her thumbs and toes were crushed in a vise, which was left in place for several hours. Finally she was whipped some more.

By the end of the day, she signed the confession that the judges demanded of her. She admitted murdering sixty infants and drinking their blood. She admitted flying on evil missions at night. And she named twenty other witches who shared these deeds with her. Once the confession was in, the judges, in good conscience, found her guilty and sentenced her to be burned at the stake.

Trials, torture, hangings, and burnings awaited people suspected of being witches. But what about those under the evil influence of the witches? How can you get rid of witches' spells, and free those possessed by the Devil? A ceremony of exorcism was devised by the Catholic Church.

Rites of Exorcism

As early as the year A.D. 250, there were exorcists working for the Church to free people from possession by the Devil. And as late as 1947, the rites of exorcism were presented in an edition of *Roman Ritual* (Benziger Brothers, New York).

The rites of exorcism are long and complex. They include many prayers, psalms, and Bible readings. Usually they begin with the priest intoning the following words: "I exorcise you, most vile spirit, the very incarnation of our adversary, the specter, the enemy, in the name of Jesus Christ, to get out and flee from this creature of God. He Himself commands you who ordered you thrown from the heights of heaven to the depths of the earth."

One of the most completely documented exorcisms took place in France in 1869. The victim was Hélène-Joséphine Poirer, who was born at Coullons on November 5, 1834.

At the age of fifteen, Hélène heard loud rapping one night, on the wall of the attic room in which she slept. Her parents, too, heard the sounds, but could not find the source. Over the following months, the girl began to suffer convulsive fits. Other physical and mental symptoms appeared.

The physicians could not find the cause of her illness. By 1864, when she was thirty years of age, it was decided that Hélène's sickness did not stem from natural causes. She was taken to a convent to be examined. The Bishop declared her to be insane, and ordered her to return home.

A few years later, Hélène wrote a statement attacking Jesus Christ and the Virgin Mary, and giving herself over to Satan. She signed the document with blood drawn from her arm. Two witnesses later claimed to have seen her rise off the ground and fly through the air. Others saw her have convulsive fits, and throw herself about in maniacal fury. During these fits, they reported, she spoke in a deep, hoarse voice, foamed at the mouth, made wild gestures, and uttered the vilest blasphemies.

In April 1869, Hélène was brought before the priests for the rites of exorcism. During the questioning, Hélène is reported to have answered in both Greek and Latin—two languages she did not speak or understand. She experienced fierce cramps and muscle spasms, howled, and made sounds like a wild animal.

The rite was pronounced five times, on five successive days. On the last day she writhed and beat around in blind fury. She cursed, she flung furniture about, and raged completely out of control. Then, she gave out one bloodcurdling shout, and collapsed. According to the account, the exorcism was successful; Hélène was free of the Devil. Although there were reported periods of possession after the exorcism, and long spells of other illnesses, Hélène lived to the age of eighty.

The highly successful novel and movie, *The Exorcist*, was based on accounts of an exorcism performed in 1949 on a fourteen-year-old boy of Mount Rainier, Washington, whose name has never been made public. The evidence of the possession was that the boy's bed would suddenly move across the room, or a chair in which he was sitting would tilt over, throwing the boy to the floor. Over a period of two months, the priests performed the ritual of exorcism more than twenty times, until in May 1949 they declared him rid of the possession.

Why Witchcraft?

Almost every period of widespread belief in witchcraft can be understood as fulfilling a need of the people in that society. That is, witchcraft may be said to be largely a creation of the men and women of a certain time, to help them to explain or accept the world in which they live.

Primitive men and women had great difficulty in understanding the world around them. Birth and death, sickness and health, storms and floods, and so on, were all baffling mysteries. They often ascribed the power to control these events to some few people among them. Very often the person chosen would be an eccentric, strange-looking man or woman who would be called a witch or a witch doctor. Later, the male witches came to be called warlocks.

Accounts indicate the belief that a good deal of the supernatural power of the witches was used for good works, or White Magic. Little was used for evil deeds, or Black Magic.

By the thirteenth century, humanity had made some progress in learning how the human body works, and about the world of nature. It was no longer as necessary to turn to magic and witchcraft for explanations. Witches, therefore, were no longer needed by society, and there began some four hundred years of persecution of witches as creatures of evil.

The Christian Church played a major role in witch hunts by claiming that witches were servants of the Devil who tried to lure souls away from the Church. Witches, the Devil, and Hell were frightening ways to keep the people faithful to the Church. Some of the most severe attacks on witches were justified on religious grounds.

By the eighteenth century, learning and understanding had spread and most people were convinced that the events that occurred around them came from completely natural causes, and had nothing to do with magical spells or potions. For the most part, the witch hunts ceased, and there was little concern with witchcraft around the world.

Since the 1960s, though, there has been a renewed interest in witchcraft. Some say that space travel, computer science, and atomic energy, as well as other advances of modern science, are so hard to understand that we long for the much simpler world of primitive magic.

Scholars have recently come up with new explanations of some of the older elements of witchcraft. For instance, it was said at the 1692 Salem trials that the witches had cast spells on some people. The symptoms of these spells were fits, odd gestures, strange postures, and garbled speech.

A modern California psychologist, Linnda R. Caporeal, writing in the April 2, 1976, issue of *Science Magazine*, gives a possible explanation of this behavior. These people, supposedly under a spell, may have been suffering from a disease called convulsive ergotism.

During a rainy season, harvested grains are sometimes infested with a type of fungus called *Claviceps purpura*, which is commonly known as ergot. Grains of ergot mix in with wheat, rye, or other grains. Included in the ergot is lysergic acid amide, a powerful drug, similar to the well-known hallucinogenic drug lysergic acid diethylamide—LSD.

Any person who eats ergot shows the symptoms of the disease convulsive ergotism. These are medically documented and include convulsions, dizziness, disturbed sensations, crawling and tingling feelings in the skin, and headaches.

The 1691 growing season in Salem was particularly rainy and warm—the best conditions for the growth of the ergot. Did an epidemic of convulsive ergotism encourage the Salem witch hunt? Did it end the following season, when the weather was dry, because there was no ergot growth?

Also, the New England colonists in America were experiencing many difficulties at that time. Relations with both England and France were strained. There was fear of attacks by Indians, taxation was very high, and pirates were interfering with shipping and trade. A smallpox epidemic killed many of the colonists and bad weather ruined much of their crops.

These problems may explain why so many colonists were willing to make victims of the witches in a desperate effort to rid themselves of their troubles.

Recent thinking may also help to explain why werewolves were so popular. Psychologists point out that people sometimes feel very powerful emotions, such as anger, hatred, or fear, that they are unable to control. At times, these emotions are so strong that they lead to animal-like behavior, such as growling, barking, whining, leaping to attack someone or cowering in fear. In the past, it may have seemed that people acting in these ways had actually become animals. It is a short step from that belief to thinking that it is possible for one person to change back and forth between the human and animal forms—to be a werewolf, vampire, or other fanciful creature.

Modern research is uncovering more and more medicinal, societal, and psychological explanations of witchcraft. Some people accept these findings, and dismiss witchcraft as an old superstition that has no place in our modern world. But there are still many who are not swayed by these arguments and place their trust in witchcraft.

9

UFOs

UFOs: *Objects seen in the air or on land that come from no known source; abbreviation for Unidentified Flying Objects.*

On June 24, 1947, a young salesman, Kenneth Arnold, was flying his private plane near Mt. Rainier, Washington. Suddenly, off in the distance, he saw nine silvery disks. They were flying through the air at a great speed, in a tight formation. The experienced pilot estimated their speed at seventeen hundred miles per hour.

Arnold reported his findings to the Yakima, Washington, Airport, saying that the planes "flew like saucers would if you skipped them across the water."

On January 7, 1948, Captain Charles Mantell was flying an F-51 plane on a routine training mission from the Godman Air Force Base in Kentucky, when he saw a large, unidentified object in the sky. He gave chase and fired at the object. Somehow, though, the object caused him to lose control of his plane and crash to the ground.

100 UFOs

On July 24, 1948, pilots Chiles and Whitted were flying an Eastern Airlines plane over Georgia when they saw a fiery-red, cigar-shaped object hurtling through space. The object came so close to their plane that the pilots were able to see windows around it. In fact, the object came so close that the pilots had to swerve their plane to avoid a collision.

In the summer of 1952, the radar screen at Washington's National Airport picked up the tracks of several objects flying overhead. The airport was closed, and jet fighters were sent up from nearby Andrews Air Force Base to investigate. They were guided to the exact location of the objects by the airport radar, but found nothing there.

On September 19, 1961, Betty and Barney Hill were driving on a deserted stretch of road through the White Mountains of New Hampshire at about three o'clock in the morning. Both husband and wife became aware of a light that followed them for several miles. Then the light pulled ahead of them and a disk-shaped object, sixty-five feet across, stopped in front of the car.

Barney later told how he got out of the car to investigate. He reported seeing humanlike figures in the craft, becoming frightened, running back to the car and driving on.

Later, the Hills realized that they could not account for a period of two hours. They both grew nervous and anxious; Barney developed an ulcer. In December 1962, they began treatment with Dr. Benjamin Simon, a psychiatrist. In the course of their treatment, Betty and Barney were hypnotized. Dr. Simon helped them to relive the missing two hours.

Under hypnosis, both Mr. and Mrs. Hill told similar stories of being brought inside the spacecraft, where they were examined by humanlike creatures. These gray-colored humanlike beings were about five feet tall, with very large eyes and almost no nose at all. At the end of the examination they were released unharmed, and told that they would forget the experience.

On December 5, 1963, the rocket-tracking cameras at Vandenberg Air Force Base in California picked up an object which could not be identified despite all efforts.

While driving near Cochrane, Wisconsin, at 8:15 P.M. on April 3, 1968, a woman and her ten-year-old son saw a shining orange object above them. It was shaped like a boomerang. At the same moment, the car engine died and the lights went out.

In fear, the woman rolled up the car windows and locked the doors. In a few minutes, the bright orange object disappeared. The woman was able to start the car and turn on the lights. She later described the sky as cloudy, with a crescent-shaped moon.

In August and September 1976, several strange objects were seen in the sky above the Hudson River, just north of New York City. One evening, Police Officer Ken Stern received a call from a twelve-year-old boy reporting an object flying above his house. When Officer

Stern arrived, he saw a round, spinning object. He examined it through his powerful field glasses, and saw that it had red, green, and white lights.

Late one afternoon, engineer-lawyer Warren Berbit saw two objects that looked like huge, upside-down soup bowls. Another time, newspaper publisher Dan Cetrone and his wife, Barbara, both reported cylindrical flying objects, also with flashing red, green, and white lights. All in all, during a three-week period around the end of August, a total of one hundred sightings were reported.

A poll of American adults conducted in 1974 showed that 11 percent of them had seen unexplained, unidentified objects in the sky, and 54 percent of the entire population believed that these objects were real. New reports of sightings still continue to come in at the rate of one hundred a day, worldwide.

At first these objects were called flying saucers because of Kenneth Arnold's description. Later reports told of differently shaped objects. People began to call them Unidentified Flying Objects or UFOs.

Since UFOs could not be identified or linked with any source on earth, it was soon widely accepted that they came from some other planet out in space. Many of the reports of sightings included "little green men" riding the UFOs.

While imaginative writers described the UFOs as visitors from outer space, the U.S. Air Force wanted to be sure that they were not an offensive weapon system being launched against the United States. In 1948, they brought together a special group of scientists and other experts at the Wright-Patterson Air Force Base at Dayton, Ohio, to investigate. Over the following twenty-one years, this group checked up on nearly thirteen thousand reports of sightings and contacts with UFOs.

In judging the reports that they received, they asked the following questions: Did the report come from the person who made the sighting or from a secondary source? Does the reporter have strong feelings either for or against UFOs? Is the observer trained in observation, such as a scientist, pilot, radar operator, or the like? Is the full description of the sighting available for further checking by investigators?

Using this approach, the experts immediately discounted about 90 percent of the reports. They found that many of these were hoaxes; the observers or the photographers had obviously faked. Some of these false reporters hoped to turn the imagined experience into a source of money; others were doing it as a joke; still others were trying to fool the experts.

A certain number of sightings were dismissed because the observer did not seem to be a reliable witness, and there was no way to check the accuracy of the report.

The rest of the discounted reports were easily explained as perfectly natural occurrences, such as airplanes or birds reflecting the sun or other light in an unusual way, peculiar cloud formations, or common optical illusions.

But what about the other 10 percent that could not be explained in any of these ways?

Most of these cases have been very thoroughly investigated. Almost every one has been explained. But these explanations have not been accepted by all. Dr. J. Allen Hynek, a professor of astronomy at Northwestern University who was involved in many of the Air Force investigations, still considers many sightings "unknown," even though other scientists consider them solved.

Here, for example, are the explanations offered for the cases listed at the beginning of this chapter:

In the Arnold case, the explanation is that the nine disks were strange reflections of the sun among the mountains.

The Captain Mantell case was solved when the Air Force authorities reported that he had been flying near a Skyhook Balloon, which measures up to one hundred feet across, and which was carrying scientific measuring instruments. At the time of the incident, this device was still secret, and Captain Mantell had no way of knowing what he was seeing. He crashed, not because he was attacked by creatures in a flying saucer, but because he flew too high and blacked out.

Several years after pilots Chiles and Whitted reported seeing a UFO from their plane, other observers described the return to earth of a Russian space satellite. It looked just like what the two pilots had seen. In fact, they probably saw a space satellite falling to earth.

As for the National Airport incident, it is believed

that the radar screen actually showed bubbles of hot air. There have been many cases of strange sightings on radar screens. They are almost always the result of unusual conditions in the atmosphere. For instance, a temperature inversion, in which hot air near the surface is trapped in place by higher cold air, often creates false images on radar screens.

Betty and Barney Hill seemed to be suffering under some sort of delusion or hallucination in their accounts of time spent in a spaceship. Yet, no one has been able to explain how both people happened to tell the same story under hypnosis.

Careful study of the films taken at Vandenberg Air Force Base shows that the camera was picking up the planet Venus, which was in that portion of the sky at the time the photographs were taken.

The clue to the explanation of the sighting by the woman and son driving in Wisconsin may be that the moon was crescent-shaped, while the UFO looked like a boomerang. The moon seen through clouds could very well have the crescent shape of a boomerang.

Dr. William Donn is head of the Atmospheric Science Program at the Lamont-Doherty Geological Observatory, which is located in the area of the 1976 sightings north of New York City. He believes that it is possible that some of the sightings were of real UFOs. "But," he said, "I can only vouch for the things I checked, and everything I investigated I identified as a bright star or a planet."

After studying some thirteen thousand cases, and

being able to explain almost every one, the Air Force dropped its investigation. They decided that there was no military danger from UFOs.

The interest in UFOs, however, and the number of sightings that are reported, continue to grow. Several private organizations are carrying on investigations, and keeping records on the sightings that are reported to them. (See list at end of book.)

The negative results of years of UFO research have convinced most nonbelievers that all sightings are either frauds, honest mistakes, or natural phenomena. Believers prefer to think that the millions of people around the world who have seen UFOs cannot all be wrong. If there are no UFOs, they ask, why can't scientists explain *every* sighting?

This leads to the heart of the entire question of UFOs, witches, ESP, and all the other "manifestations of the supernatural": Can we be sure either that these things exist or that they do not exist?

One group holds that there still is not enough valid, objective evidence to prove the existence or the nonexistence of the supernatural. They want much more research on all aspects of the supernatural and occult. Then each person will have the facts and figures on which to base an informed decision.

Another position has been well stated by William James, the famous psychologist. It is only necessary, he said, to find one white crow to disprove the statement that all crows are black. Therefore, if there is just one accepted example of the supernatural, one must accept the existence of the supernatural.

A third view has been put forth by The Amazing Randi, the well-known magician and debunker of psychics. Most people, he points out, do not believe in Santa Claus, since they know who gives them the gifts that they receive at Christmas. Even if they did not know who gave them one of their gifts, this would not lead them to believe in Santa Claus. Since most supernatural events can be explained in a natural way, that is enough reason for one not to accept the existence of the supernatural.

SOME BOOKS OF INTEREST

ESP and Parapsychology

Ebon, Martin, ed. *Test Your ESP.* New York: T. Y. Crowell, 1970.
> Many ESP activities and games.

Hansel, C. E. M. *ESP: A Scientific Evaluation.* New York: Scribner's, 1966.
> The famous book offering arguments against ESP.

Pratt, Joseph Gaither. *Parapsychology: An Insider's View of ESP.* New York: Dutton, 1966.

Rhine, J. B. *New Frontiers of the Mind.* New York: Farrar and Rinehart, 1937.

Rhine, Louisa E. *Mind Over Matter.* New York: Macmillan, 1970.
> Three important books by leaders of the Duke Parapsychology Laboratory.

Rogo, D. Scott. *Parapsychology.* New York: Dell, 1975.
> A thorough book by a leading researcher.

Astrology

Adams, Evangeline. *Astrology: Your Place Among the Stars*. New York: Dodd, Mead, 1930.
   A classic book on astrology.
Davison, Ronald C. *Astrology*. New York: Arco, 1963.
   Instructions on casting your own horoscope.
McIntosh, Christopher. *The Astrologers and Their Creed*. New York: Praeger, 1969.
   Scholarly history of astrology.

Psychokinesis

The Amazing Randi. *The Magic of Uri Geller*. New York: Ballantine Books, 1975.
   Explanations of PK as magicians' tricks.
Christopher, Milbourne. *Mediums, Mystics and the Occult*. New York: T. Y. Crowell, 1975.
   Discussions of Margery and Geller.
Geller, Uri. *My Story*. New York: Praeger, 1975.
   A full account by one of the world's most famous psychics.

Spiritualism

Christopher, Milbourne. *Mediums, Mystics and the Occult*. New York: T. Y. Crowell, 1975.
   A stage magician exposes frauds among Spiritualists.
McHargue, Georges. *Facts, Frauds and Phantasms*. Garden City: Doubleday, 1972.
   A history of Spiritualism.

Stemman, Roy. *Spirits and Spirit Worlds*. Garden City: Doubleday, 1976.
   Illustrated survey of Spiritualism.

Faith Healing

Fuller, John G. *Arigo: Surgeon of the Rusty Knife*. New York: T. Y. Crowell, 1974.
   Account of a Brazilian psychic surgeon.
Rose, Louis. *Faith Healing*. Hammondsworth, England: Penguin, 1971.
   A psychiatrist reports studies on faith healing.
St. Clair, David. *Psychic Healers*. Garden City: Doubleday, 1974.
   Accounts of work of eleven American faith healers.

Witchcraft

Epstein, Perle. *The Way of Witches*. Garden City: Doubleday, 1972.
   General book on witchcraft.
Farrar, Stewart. *What Witches Do*. New York: Coward McCann, 1971.
   First-person account of a British coven.
Gibson, Walter B. *Witchcraft*. New York: Grosset and Dunlap, 1973.
   General book on witchcraft.
Heriot, John. *Teaching Yourself White Magic*. New York: A. S. Barnes, 1973.
   Do-it-yourself witchcraft.

Some Books of Interest

LaVey, Anton Szandor. *The Satanic Bible*. New York: Avon, 1969.
> The Bible of the West Coast Churches of Satan.

Murray, Margaret Alice. *The Witch-Cult in Western Europe*. Oxford, England: Oxford, 1962.
> A classic history of witchcraft.

Smyth, Frank. *Modern Witchcraft*. New York: Harrow, 1973.
> Witchcraft as practiced today.

Summers, Montague. *The History of Witchcraft*. Secaucus, N.J.: Citadel, 1971.
> A classic history of witchcraft.

UFOs

Hynek, J. Allen and Vallee, Jacques. *The Edge of Reality*. Chicago: Regnery, 1975.
> Two researchers convinced of reality of UFOs.

Menzel, Donald H. and Boyd, Lyle G. *The World of Flying Saucers*. Garden City: Doubleday, 1963.
> Two researchers who do not believe in UFOs.

Sagan, Carl and Page, Thornton. *UFOs—A Scientific Debate*. Ithaca, N.Y.: Cornell, 1972.
> Many different viewpoints on UFOs.

SOME ADDRESSES OF INTEREST

*For information on parapsychology,
and to report high ESP test scores:*

American Society for Psychical Research
5 West 73rd Street
New York, N.Y. 10023

Institute for Parapsychology
Box 6847
College Station
Durham, North Carolina 27706

Parapsychology Foundation
29 West 57th Street
New York, N.Y. 10019

Parapsychology Research Foundation
Box 6116
Duke Station
Durham, North Carolina 27706

113 Some Addresses of Interest

To report premonitions:

    Central Premonitions Registry
    Box 482
    Times Square Station
    New York, N.Y. 10036

    Premonitions Registry
    Toronto Society for Psychical Research
    10 N. Sherbourne Street
    Toronto 5, Ontario, Canada

For information on astrology:

    National Astrological Society
    127 Madison Avenue
    New York, N.Y. 10016

For information on Spiritualism:

    National Spiritualist Association of Churches
    P.O. Box 128
    Cassadaga, Florida 32706

For information on faith healing:

    Spiritual Frontiers Fellowship
    800 Custer Avenue
    Evanston, Illinois 60202

Some Addresses of Interest

For information on UFOs, and to report sightings:

Center for UFO Studies
P.O. Box 11
Northfield, Illinois 60093

INDEX

Adams, Evangeline, 31-32, 33, 36
Agpaoa, Antonio, 77-79
Association for Research and Enlightenment, 9
astrology, 30-46

Black Mass, 90
Blackburn, Douglas, 16-18, 25
blindfold, 14-15

Cayce, Edgar, 8-9
clairaudience, 8
clairvoyance, 7, 22, 27
    tests of, 12-13
Cone of Power, 85
convulsive ergotism, 96-97
coven, 84, 85, 86
Crandon, Mina, *see* Margery
cusps, 37-39

Davis, Andrew Jackson, 69
decans, 37, 40-41
dreams, 29

Edwards, Harry, 79-80, 81
esbat, 84
ESP, 4-15
    deceptive, 14-15
    experiments, 19-24
    improvement of, 13-14
    tests of, 11-13
exorcism, 92-95
extrasensory perception, *see* ESP

faith healing, 75-82
flying saucers (*see also* UFOs), 99, 102
Ford, Arthur, 69-72, 73

fortune telling (see also astrology), 45-46
Fox, Margaret and Kate, 64-68

Geller, Uri, 52-59
grimoires, 86, 88

horoscope, 36-43
Houdini, Harry, 49-52, 70-71
Hurkos, Peter, 8

I Ching, 45
imagery, 87-88
inspirational talk, 63

LaVey, Anton, 87
Linzmayer, Adam J., 20-21, 26
lycanthropy, see werewolves

magic, 87-88
  black, 86, 88, 95
  white, 85, 86, 88, 95
magicians, 55-59, 82
Margery, 48-52
Mark of the Devil, 86-87, 91
McDougall, William, 19
mediums, 48, 61-63, 66-67, 72-74
mental message (see also telepathy), 2
Message Service, 60-63
mind reading, see telepathy

National Spiritualist Association of Churches, 64, 69-70, 72-74

Occult Investigation Committee, 55

parapsychology, 16-29
  research in, centers for, 19-23, 28-29
Parapsychology Laboratory, Duke University, 19-23
Pearce-Platt experiments, 21-22, 26
Pike, James A., 71-72
PK, see psychokinesis
planetary influence (see also astrology), 39-40
precognition, 7-8, 22
  test of, 13
psi, 19, 20, 21, 22, 23
psychics, 10, 47, 48-49, 55
psychokinesis, 8, 22, 27, 47-59
psychosurgery, 77-79, 82
pyramids, 85

retrocognition, 8
Rhine, Joseph Banks, 19-28
Rhine, Louisa, 19
Rose, Louis, 80-81

Schmeidler, Gertrude, 23

Index

séances (*see also* Spiritualism), 49-50
second sight, *see* clairvoyance
sensory cues, 9-10, 13, 27
Smith, George Albert, 16-18, 25
Society for Psychical Research, 17-18
Spiritualism, 60-74

tarot cards, 45
telekinesis, *see* psychokinesis
telepathy, 7, 16-19, 22, 27, 29
    tests of, 11-12

UFOs, 99-107

Unidentified Flying Objects, *see* UFOs
U.S. Air Force, and UFOs, 102-106

Van Damm, A., 18-19, 25-26

werewolves, 89-90, 97-98
witchcraft, 83-98
    and Christianity, 90-95, 96

witch hunts, 86-87, 90-92, 95-96
    in Salem, 97

Zener cards, 20, 22, 27
Zodiac signs, 33-35

About the Author

Melvin Berger is the author of over thirty books on science for young readers. A number of his books, including *Oceanography Lab, Pollution Lab* and *Consumer Protection Labs,* have been chosen as Outstanding Science Books for Children by the National Science Teachers Association and the Children's Book Council.

Mr. Berger was educated at City College of New York; University of Rochester, where he received his bachelor's degree; Columbia University, where he received his master's degree; and London University. He lives with his wife and two daughters in Great Neck, New York.

**LEW WALLACE
HIGH SCHOOL·LIBRARY**